English and Ability

Edited by Andrew Goodwyn

David Fulton Publishers Ltd
2 Barbon Close, London WC1N 3JX

First published in Great Britain by
David Fulton Publishers 1995

Note: The right of Andrew Goodwyn to be identified as the editor of this work
has been asserted by him in accordance with the Copyright, Designs and
Patents Act 1988.

Copyright © David Fulton Publishers Ltd

British Library Cataloguing in Publication Data

A catalogue record for this book is available from the British Library

ISBN 1-85346-299-3

Typeset by Harrington & Co
Printed in Great Britain by BPC Books and Journals, Exeter.

Contents

Dedication

To Tom and Helena Goodwyn

Acknowledgements

I should like to thank the pupils and staff, and especially the English Departments, of Kendrick School, Yateley School and Bulmershe School for their help with the research; also the following former student teachers who helped with the research – Trudy Bell, Louisa Bray, Claire Carter, Debra Elvin, Suzanne Grant, Angela Hazel, Les Lanagan, Sarah Munday and Nancy Robinson.

I also thank all the contributors for their hard work and ability to meet deadlines and, my patient and faithful editor, John Owens.

Foreword

The original idea for this collection of seven essays was to explore the concept of ability in English, an elusive concept about which there are probably many differing opinions within the English teaching profession itself. What seems clear from the available research, however, is that English teachers do share an intensely optimistic view of human capacity and potential, with ability as some form of simple, measurable entity having little place in their thinking about pupils' learning. In the case of poetry, for example, there is a general concern to respect the original and the creative, without risking the damage that could be caused by the impression of crude assessment procedures.

All the contributors to this thought-provoking volume agree that ability in English is a complex, dynamic element where the search for definitive, once-and-for-all tests is a fruitless activity. Ability in English is seen to be about the development of individual pupils in particular social and cultural contexts, with teachers having to be constantly aware of the wide range of variables that affect progress. Since ability in English is such a complex matter, we obviously need to create assessment procedures that are sufficiently flexible to acknowledge the centrality of the individual pupil and, at the same time, enable teachers to make genuinely diagnostic evaluations in favourable day-to-day situations and across a range of contexts.

Clyde Chitty
Birmingham
October 1994

QUALITY IN SECONDARY SCHOOLS AND COLLEGES SERIES

Series Editor, Clyde Chitty

This new series publishes on a wide range of topics related to successful education for the 11-19 age group. It reflects the growing interest in whole-school curriculum planning, together with the effective teaching of individual subjects and themes. There will also be books devoted to management and administration, examinations and assessment, pastoral care strategies, relationships with parents and governors and the implications for schools of changes in teacher education.

Early titles include:

Active History in Key Stages 3 and 4
Alan Farmer and Peter Knight
1-85346-305-1

English and the OFSTED Experience
Bob Bibby, Barrie Wade and Trevor Dickinson
1-85346-357-4

English as a Creative Art
Linden Peach and Angela Burton
1-85346-368-X

Geography 11-16: Rediscovering Good Practice
Bill Marsden
1-85346-296-9

The Literate Imagination: Renewing the Secondary English Curriculum
Bernard T. Harrison
1-85346-300-0

Moral Education through English 11-16
Ros McCulloch and Margaret Mathieson
1-85346-276-4

Partnership in Secondary Teacher Education
Edited by Anne Williams
1-85346-361-2

Shaping Secondary Schooling: Talking with Headteachers
Edited by David Hustler, John Robinson and Tim Brighouse
1-85346-358-2

Preface

Since the inception of the National Curriculum the school subject known loosely as 'English' has been subjected to intensive and frequently hostile scrutiny. Many individuals and pressure groups have pronounced on what English should be like and, most often, how it should be assessed. These pronouncements are usually based on the misconception of returning to a so called 'old fashioned' and simpler form of English teaching. This book is not aimed at such people who have no faith in the subject as it is currently taught. Instead it is intended to help those who actually work with children or students or teachers or all three and who believe that we are actually doing a good job teaching English but recognise, of course, that we would like to improve.

One potential improvement would be a clearer view of what 'being good at English' actually means and that is what this book attempts to provide. The contributors to this volume come at the topic from a variety of directions but all with the intention of helping us towards a better appreciation of how we can understand ability in English and support children's development. The book avoids some of the particularly obscuring aspects of the National Curriculum in English and concentrates on what really counts, how teachers and children learn in the classroom.

Andrew Goodwyn
Reading,
October 1994

List of Contributors

Judith Baxter is a Lecturer in English and Education at the University of Reading. She is also Series Editor of *Cambridge Literature for Schools*.

Becky Green is an English teacher, currently second in the English Department at Bemrose School in Derby.

Andrew Goodwyn has been a Lecturer in English in Education at the University of Reading since 1988, following twelve years teaching English in a range of secondary schools and colleges in the UK and the USA, culminating in four years as Head of English at an 11–16 comprehensive school. He has edited and written a number of anthologies, pupil materials and books for English teachers, as well as numerous reviews, journal articles and chapters in contributed books.

Sallyanne Greenwood has been a Lecturer in the School of Education at Nottingham University since 1989. She has also worked as an English teacher, a National Writing Project Co-ordinator and TVEI advisory teacher.

Colin Harrison is Reader in Education at Nottingham University. His main research interests are in reading development, assesssment and new technology. He has become increasingly interested in the politics of literacy and assessment, and serves on the International Reading Association's Family Literacy Commission.

Alan Howe is currently an English Consultant with Wiltshire LEA. He was Director of the Wiltshire Oracy Project from 1983–90, and a Project Officer from 1990–92. He has written extensively about oracy, including *Making Talk Work* (1992) and *Common Bonds – Storytelling in the Classroom* (with John Johnson, 1993).

Robert Protherough was formerly at the University of Hull and has been one of the most significant contributors to the field of English in education both in the United Kingdom and abroad.

CHAPTER 1

Introduction: Contextualising ability within the subject of English

The school subject of English has never had such a high profile in the United Kingdom as it achieved in the 1980s and 1990s. It has become a subject besieged by politicians of all parties, influential pressure groups of all kinds, government agencies and quangos, the media, parents – the list is endless. Every formal document about English tends to begin with the point that English is the most important of all school subjects and so getting English right is seen as vital to the future of the nation – a claim made consistently since the Newbolt Report in 1922. This point is curiously uncontentious! Even teachers of other subjects do not oppose such high status for English – the one actual consensus about English is that English matters most. Robert Protherough summarises a great deal of research in his *Students of English* (1989), showing how various studies suggest that school leavers rated English as the most important subject and that all pupils considered that it offered most social benefit. English is unique in being perceived by pupils as interesting and entertaining and, if it is helpfully and clearly explained, pupils in general feel that both the subject matter and the teachers are interesting.

However, such universally approved status means that, outside the professional community of English teachers and researchers, every other aspect of English as a school subject is highly contentious. Every subject expects to have internal differences and disagreements expressed by its practitioners but others do not receive such a barrage of versions of what 'getting it right' would mean.

Because English involves both the use of and the study of the four language modes, *speaking* and *listening*, *reading* and *writing*, it can never be a subject with neatly drawn boundaries. 'Whereas the acquisition of most subjects begins and ends with the teaching of that subject in school, children bring to English a wealth of existing language experience and the boundaries of what they do in it through English have no fixed limits' (Protherough 1989).

Pupils use these language modes not only throughout the school but also throughout ordinary life and so the content of English is determined by a selection from a vast range of possible aspects of language. This selection is, in effect, a privileging of certain aspects of the four language modes – for example, particular kinds of writing. As an instance, pupils are encouraged to write poetry (and to read it) and this type of writing is seen as exclusively the province of English. The essay on the other hand has a place in many other school subjects. However, the essay is frequently used in several subjects, both in examinations and coursework, as a measure of ability in the subject itself. Yet, although poetry is a distinct element of English, there are no measures in the National Curriculum of poetic ability.

I am highlighting the immense complexity of factors affecting notions of the subject English and also, therefore, of what ability in English might mean. It is not that poetry writing is unconnected to some kind of ability; it is much more to do with the powerful cultural and historical pressures bearing down upon both the reading and writing of poetry that mean that teachers and pupils engage with poetry within a predetermined and hierarchical structure, making poetry teaching remarkably problematic (Andrews 1991).

Models of English and Models of Ability

In the English teaching profession there are no doubt many differing views about what ability in English might mean but it is highly significant that the issue of ability itself does not seem to generate much debate. There does seem to be a reasonable consensus amongst teachers about their rationale for English, and research suggests (Goodwyn 1992) that the Cox Report, to a large extent, got it right in putting forward a description of the four models that operate within the subject. One major reason for this lack of contention is that the model of English which predominates has been consistently in place for the last thirty years. This model, the Personal Growth model of English as defined by the Cox Committee for example (DES 1989, 2.21), explains that:

A 'personal growth' view focuses on the child: it emphasises the relationship between language and learning in the individual child, and the role of literature in developing children's imaginative and aesthetic lives.

It is not concerned with a concept of ability but with the development of the individual.

> English teachers…see themselves as more widely concerned with students as developing individuals than with particular subject matter. The emphasis in English is on personal experiences, on the affective inseparable from the cognitive, contributing to learning in all areas of the curriculum and of life. (Protherough 1989, p.8.)

This model offers an essentially non-competitive, non-hierarchical approach to the subject. It is not concerned with linear progression but much more with a widening spiral notion of development in which the individual steadily improves over the four language modes but within that improvement there is a constant recursion and stimulation of various kinds, including teaching, which may lead to sudden spurts of growth. The Cox Report stressed this point (DES 1989, 14.5):

> We acknowledge the problems in defining a linear sequence of development, which has been the subject of a great deal of research. This has shown that children do not learn particular features of, for example, written language, once and for all at any particular stage; they continually return to the same features and refine their competence.

However the Cultural Heritage model is very different and offers a quite distinct emphasis from Personal Growth, (DES 1989, 2.24):

> A 'cultural heritage' view emphasises the responsibility of schools to lead children to an appreciation of those works of literature that have been widely regarded as amongst the finest in the language.

From one perspective it is simply about acquiring as much cultural capital as possible and so ability involves straightforward acquisition; something easily measured by volume – how many 'finest works' has each child appreciated. However, this model is the least important for English teachers (Goodwyn 1992) except when related to Personal Growth as it then provides a means by which individuals who may feel affinities with several cultures can come to terms with the predominant heritage and find meaning in it. Cultural Heritage is clearly the key model for certain pressure groups, all of whom tend to look backward to a time of imaginary cultural unity. However, this model in isolation is not concerned with growth but is almost entirely static; culture already exists as a finished entity and pupils have to become acquainted with it.

The model which is, in a sense, currently gaining ground, is Cultural Analysis and it provides a bridge between the two discussed above (DES 1989, 2.25).

A 'cultural analysis' view emphasises the role of English in helping children towards a critical understanding of the world and cultural environment in which they live. Children should know about the processes by which meanings are conveyed, and about the ways in which print and other media carry values.

Here the stress is on a broad understanding of texts, an openness to questioning and interpretation and knowledge about the social production of meaning. Analysis is the key factor and the Personal Growth element keeps the emphasis, as in Reader Response theories, on how each individual generates and refines a meaningful response. Pupils do not inherit a culture, they are already a part of it and what they have to do is locate themselves, and others, within a framework, partly historical, in which culture becomes meaningful.

The other prominent model of English is Adult Needs. This model lays stress on outcomes rather than abilities (DES 1989, 2.23).

An adult needs view focuses on communication outside the school: it emphasises the responsibility of English teachers to prepare children for the language demands of adult life, including the work-place, in a fast-changing world. Children need to learn to deal with the day-to-day demands of spoken language and of print; they also need to be able to write clearly, appropriately and effectively.

The underlying principle is that pupils should be competent in the adult world and particularly the world of work and as an agent in society. Its emphasis is on a kind of communicative competence. It stresses, as do employers generally, the ability to talk to and work with others. The only way to assess an individual in school is through a whole range of differing tasks, some of which would necessarily involve role play or simulations in order to provide an imitation of an adult world context.

English teachers agree (Goodwyn 1992) on the value of all these models but they place Personal Growth first and Cultural Analysis second and so ability as some kind of simple, measurable quality has little place in their thinking about pupils' learning. The question that we lack a neat answer to as yet is, 'So what exactly is growth?'. There have been many studies of this concept of growth and the majority have focussed on responsiveness to literature (Protherough 1983, 1986) and on defining stages of reader responsiveness (Thomson 1987, Appleyard 1990). Other chapters in this book also consider answers to that question with emphases on different aspects of the subject or of the way it is organised in school.

One aspect of Personal Growth, touched on in the Cox Committee's definition – 'the role of literature in developing children's imaginative and aesthetic lives' – is more problematic and deserves some particular consideration at this point. One strand in the subject of English can be traced back to the Romantic movement and its privileging of the original, creative artist. In this view of Art, genius comes entirely from within and is defined as separate from the conventional and sordid ordinariness of most human life (Eagleton 1983). The Romantic concept offers us all the hope that we may have some of this genius within us but it also implies that we typically allow our potential as children to wither – we become very uncreative adults. One institutionalised result of this is that we can become critics instead. The history of English 'A' level, excluding perhaps parts of the 1980s, demonstrates how students are expected to become appreciators of genius and not creative artists themselves.

What this strand highlights is the problem of 'originality'; how does originality relate to ability? Poetry provides a useful way to consider this problem. Research has revealed (DES 1987, Benton 1988) that English teachers have generally been reluctant to teach poetry to 11–16 year olds; it makes them feel uncomfortable and there is a suggestion that some teachers feel as if the pupils rather contaminate this specially precious form of language. However, pupils are often encouraged to write poetry and children are regularly praised for their gift in this area and even for their originality. However, as Cox put it (DES 1989, 17.29), no one should have to write a poem: 'we have not included a poetry strand in the statements of attainment because we do not feel that any pupil should be *required* to write a poem in order to achieve a particular level of attainment'.

My own research with student teachers over the last three years has shown how they consistently shy away from assessing poetry, they want to value it and to respond to it but they would never wish to assess it. This reluctance to assess reveals a deep concern in English teachers to revere the creative and the original and not to damage it by assessment. Again we see how ability is not a simple issue for the English teacher. The encouragement of the individual's capacity to produce poetic language is far more important than any teacher judgement or measurement. It is also clear that such ability is perceived as potentially inherent in all pupils at all times. There is a sense in which this is an intensely optimistic view of human capacity and English teachers do consistently rate their pupils' abilities higher than do teachers in other subjects (Protherough 1989, p.8).

To sum up so far, teachers of English – who actually carry out pupil assessment, whoever else may think that they control the assessment – are working with a composite model made up from the complex interrelationship between four important models of English. As Personal Growth colours everything that they do, so it becomes essential to view ability in the subject as a complex, dynamic element, more of a process than a simple, observable product.

So what counts as ability in English?

The reason for the preponderance of contention, see above, rather than agreement about English is not solely to do with content and has enormous implications for what counts as ability in English. Two specific examples are worth using as illustrations of the complexity of the concept in English. These examples, spoken English and Shakespeare, have been chosen as they always raise so much heat but also because the former illustrates issues to do with teaching about language, and the latter, teaching about literature.

There is absolute agreement that English should involve the study of the language called English (DES 1989, 2.13).

> The overriding aim of the English curriculum is to enable all pupils to develop to the full their ability to use and understand English. Since language can be both spoken and written, this means the fullest possible development of capabilities in speaking and listening, reading and writing.

All parties agree that some of this study will be devoted to written Standard English and some to formal and informal modes of speaking. However, there all agreement ends.

The current pressure on the curriculum since the proposed changes to the National Curriculum put forward in 1993 (DFE 1993, SCAA 1994) has been to make Standard English into a fixed part of assessment. The National Curriculum levels would contain linguistic markers preventing pupils from achieving higher levels if they failed to use certain forms of speech deemed to be spoken Standard English. The proposed Level Description for Level 4 states, 'They use some of the core features of Standard English vocabulary and grammar appropriately' (p.30). This would include, according to the Programme of Study (p.5), 'consistent use of verb tenses and subject–verb agreement: correct standard forms of negatives, plurals and pronouns'. In other words the test of ability would become the pupil's capacity to speak exactly the same as every other pupil in the country is supposed to do; the fact that neither children nor adults speak like this is apparently unimportant.

An opposite view (DES 1989, Chapter 4) put forward about Spoken Standard English is that pupils should, where appropriate, gradually add the formal registers of English to their more everyday ones. Here the stress is on developing a broad awareness of how English works and being able to use it effectively in a range of situations. The ability tested here is harder to define narrowly as it involves sensitivity to language and knowledge about how it works. Such an ability would place stress on the pupil's competence in adjusting language use to fit varied and varying situations – in other words an individual could not be tested on speaking the same as the rest of the nation because we know, empirically, that the nation has different ways of speaking in different parts of the country.

Another topic which all parties welcome is the study of Shakespeare but, again, the agreement ends there. Over the last twenty years there has been a steady movement away from what might be termed a desk-bound approach to Shakespeare's plays. The desk-bound approach involved reading every word of the play around the class and then going over the play again in verbal detail but rarely treating the text as a play. This approach was assessed through essays often depending on memorised quotations. Many teachers are currently using drama techniques as well as close reading and involving pupils in interpreting the text dramatically; that is, just as actors and directors do, exploring the text to make it meaningful. They begin with a text and read it closely but they must engage with its purpose which is to be enacted.

These differing approaches have implicit within them different models of reading ability and, even more crucially, of what it is worth understanding about Shakespeare. The first one requires pupils to commit much of the text to memory and to be able to produce an appreciation of the text, often more as a poem than as a play; this reflects the narrowest definition of Cultural Heritage. It has tended to mean pupils learning set answers to predictable questions and, through judicious application of examination techniques, ensuring that they please the examiner. 'With a good memory, a good teacher and no feeling at all for the subject, it is possible to get high grades' (quoted in Protherough 1986).

The more drama based approach implies developing an understanding of what kind of play Shakespeare was trying to write; it also implies developing a much more individual view because pupils have to interpret the text (Cultural Analysis) rather than passively appreciate it – appreciation comes through enactment. Finally the models of ability involve different views of enjoyment and pleasure in the work. The desk-bound model has placed little value on enjoying the text whereas the drama approach has provided numerous opportunities for pupils to become actively engaged in enjoying the text through interpreting it. English teachers always rate enjoyment very highly as an objective in their teaching (Yorke 1974, 1976).

What these two examples are intended to highlight is that we cannot examine ability in a subject like English in any simplistic way. Because English is tied in to every individual's use of language there can be no simple means of grading those individuals. In fact the crucial element is to move away from looking for the perfect test of ability in English. That is a chimera. The important step forward is to identify broad areas where progress can be made and to recognise the range of variables that affect that progress. For example, if pupils are to enjoy or appreciate literature, then no test on earth can make them have these experiences. If pupils are to become confident and fluent users of English, then it must be vital that they are not discouraged from constantly using the language through fear of failing whenever they open their mouths.

Ability in English is about the development of the individual in a social and cultural context and cannot be reduced to less than this complex inter-action. The subject of English is concerned with human beings' collective and individual use of language, something that is constantly changing and developing. It is inevitably, and properly, much easier to understand how well a child is developing as a language user through monitoring that development over time but without impeding it by being over concerned with products. Someone who has ability in English has the capacity to receive and produce language with an increasing awareness of that lan-guage and of his or her individual relationship to it.

Assessment in English

Similarly, assessment in English is by subjective individuals who draw on personal and collective expertise to reach agreements about the progress individuals have made and maintained and usually demonstrated through reading, writing, speaking and listening. Most public examining in English up until the advent first of CSE and then GCSE had depended on the simplistic notion that if you send a pupil's examination answers to an English teacher who does not know the pupil, then that assessor's judge-ment will be highly objective. All it is is anonymous! That judgement is then cross-checked by another judgement and then either confirmed or altered. A social factor in all this is that examiners undertake their task for piece-work payments, usually at the exhausted end of the academic year and to meet incredibly tight deadlines.

The original GCSE system, using 100% coursework, had modified this system so the initial teacher's original judgements were then moderated within the institution by another colleague who knew the context, i.e. who had valuable local knowledge to employ in making judgements. These two judgements were then moderated by another teacher external to the school as a part of a sample of schools, that moderator having the power to insist on changes to all grades from the school. In other words if the school was too soft or too hard, or simply inconsistent, they might affect the results of all their pupils. This was real collective responsibility.

This was not a perfect system because there cannot be one but it did combine the element of objectification with the powerful addition of contextual knowledge. It also achieved two remarkable and positive changes. First, it demystified examining to teachers and pupils; it was an open and understood process. Second, it created a wealth of assessment expertise in every school. As all teachers could be involved, so they were becoming increasingly clear about what they valued in a pupil's progress and this could connect to their teaching. This practise in refining subjective judgement was having a beneficial effect on good practice in the classroom. The steady rise in GCSE results in English and in pupils staying on to study the subject, suggests that standards were genuinely rising during the period of greatest teacher involvement in the assessment of English.

It becomes increasingly clear then that ability in English is not so much a problematic concept as a valuably complicated concept. English teachers themselves are quite happy with a holistic and broad approach to assessment which they see as vital if it is to be possible to assess pupils' ability in English and to reward their individual achievements. Examinations and tests are very limited and limiting and do not provide a broad, holistic framework for assessment.

One important point is an increasing preponderance of evidence that shows that ability is a potentially misleading term in a more general sense. In the complex modern world and in the increasingly complex modern school perceptions certainly count for as much if not more when it comes to understanding how pupils achieve success on anyone's terms, including their own (Johnston 1987). Coursework was an especially effective way of improving pupils' self-awareness and their ability to reflect on their own and others' progress. If assessment is to be effective generally, it needs to involve and include pupils themselves and in English, a subject that makes pre-eminent both the person and the personal, it is absolutely paramount. If assessment in English returns to a simplistic model of heritage based on an absurdly limited definition of culture that incorporates a static view of Standard English, then a pupils' actual ability in the subject will have little to do with any 'results'.

A good example to focus on in this section is spelling, a feature of English that all agree is important but problematic (see Chapter 2). It seems that there is a strong correlation between achieving a high level of correct spelling and a belief in the individual that they can achieve this level (Peters 1987). I have yet to teach a pupil who wants to misspell words. Even the most apparently wilful of spellers is simply making mistakes and admits to being 'bad at spelling'. Equally I have not encountered any human being, even those with high status jobs in industry or several university degrees, who was sure about the spelling of every word; this point is hardly a revelation to the reader but it is an important reminder, nevertheless.

Spelling is an important element in written communication and the majority of individuals make reasonable progress in learning how to accomplish it, but they never finish learning. It is an element that you can, as a teacher, isolate and concentrate upon but it is not an ability in any pure sense that is the foundation for writing. Recent moves to take marks off for spelling mistakes in examinations are therefore a rather curious move. They might well be justified on the basis of measuring a writer's attention to and care with language. Why then is this ability to be tested under the stress of examination conditions which in no way mirror adult models of writing? Any adult writing something important tries to take their time and to draft and check their work before committing it to the intended audience.

It is notable that almost all efforts by English teachers have been to help pupils to produce formally assessed work under 'normal conditions' and it is particularly striking that the Assessment of Performance Unit adopted this approach. As Myra Barrs (Barrs 1990) expresses it:

It is now generally accepted that the sampling of normal behaviour in favourable day-to-day contexts is likely to give a better and more reliable picture of a child or a student's capabilities as a language learner than that which emerges from a one-off assessment in an unfamiliar situation.

The fact that some individuals may choose to isolate spelling as a means by which to select another individual, for example for a job, is an important social fact but it is not a recognition of that individual's capacity to use language or read texts. Pupils are entirely convinced of the importance of spelling, see Chapter 2.

We need to understand why English teachers, those people whose daily lives are devoted to helping children develop as understanders of and as users of English, do value spelling but never to the exclusion of much else that is crucial. Assessment in English would appear extremely silly, even to those who are particularly concerned with spelling, if spelling was the measure by which a student's writing was judged. In a curious way the removal of only a few marks recognises this point. Holistic and longitudinal assessment would allow someone to judge the relative spelling ability of any pupil and, if poor, to what extent it consistently interfered with meaning. Assessment of ability in English can be accurate only over time, allowing a teacher time to make a genuinely diagnostic evaluation.

Attempts to measure achievement in language analytically have increasingly come to appear less convincing because of the growing recognition that the processes to be assessed are complex and that analytic forms of assessment used are often too crude to be useful...The problem with analytic approaches to assessment in language is that they usually rest on inadequate models of language, and they do not recognise that, even if it were possible to break language processes down in some way or to identify sets of sub-skills, what counts as competence is the way in which a reader or writer is able to orchestrate these skills in a particular performance. (Barrs 1990.)

Myra Barrs puts forward seven principles that should allow us to recognise achievement in English and to make judgements about ability.

1. The assessment of normal behaviour in favourable contexts.
2. The importance of assessment across a range of contexts.
3. The assessment of process as well as product.
4. The holistic assessment of complex processes.
5. The sharing of criteria with students.
6. The inclusion of pupils' self-assessment.
7. Equality in assessment. (Barrs 1990, pp. 34-39.)

These points complement the work of Johnston (1987) whose earlier book had many valuable points to make about a workable approach to assessment in English.

Current proposed changes to the National Curriculum for English are in great danger of ruining the work of many years' thorough research and steadily improving classroom practice. Teacher assessment in English is vital and can be steadily improved through moderation work across the four language modes.

Towards a Conclusion

The original idea for this collection was to explore the concept of ability in English, to examine and appraise what we feel we know about this concept and to offer some help and guidance. There was never any intention to provide a unanimous view through oversimplifying the issues. However, the different chapters, whilst focussing on particular areas and showing a range of views, all complement and add to one another and provide a remarkably consistent attitude.

In Chapter 2, I examine what 'being good at English' means to English teachers and their pupils. We find that there is a common understanding between them about the purpose and value of the subject and about the characteristics of successful pupils. I am able to offer some views about the most able in English and about how we might support their development.

In Judy Baxter's chapter on mixed ability we find evidence of the restrictive pressure of the National Curriculum beginning to distort good practice. It clearly is important that English Departments review what they mean by mixed ability but the chapter also shows why many English teachers remain convinced that this approach is the best on educational grounds as it genuinely raises expectations and standards.

Robert Protherough's chapter on writing reinforces my points above about subjectivity. He points out that, however wished for, there are no tidy and simple ways to assess writing ability, it is not a unitary concept and it is usually the assessment procedure itself that determines what is valued. He shows how constant public anxiety about standards in schools had prevented the development of an effective assessment system until the arrival of coursework and how we are now heading back towards that reductive approach. His review of the research leaves us in no doubt about the entirely negative effects that will follow if the current proposals about writing become enshrined in the National Curriculum.

Colin Harrison complements Robert Protherough's ideas by focussing on the literal impossibility of getting directly at someone's ability to read. We approach it only through another medium, such as writing. Ability in reading is even more problematic than writing because it is bound up with political, social and cultural power. He places the individual at the heart of reading assessment, stressing the validity of the reading interview as a means of building up a real knowledge of the strategies that readers themselves bring to texts.

Colin Harrison's stress on making the assessment of reading meaningful to the reader ties in with Alan Howe's view that speaking and listening are not divisible from the context in which they take place. Development through talk can happen only through a gradual increase in the repertoire of speakers and through the encouragement of versatility. He rejects the reductive view that simply equates oral proficiency with talking at larger and larger audiences.

Finally Sallyanne Greenwood and Becky Green provide a thorough examination of low achievers in English. They complement my earlier points about the key place played by perceptions of ability. Low achievers tend to develop a theory not of personal growth but of inevitable personal failure and the pressures of the National Curriculum, which the authors see as competitive and hierarchical, reinforce these theories. When these pupils are asked to identify what matters in English they refer only to the mechanistic and surface features of language, so trapping themselves in a particularly limiting model of language.

All the chapters stress the centrality of the individual pupil and the need for a system of teaching and assessment that constantly acknowledge this crucial principle. Pupils need equal access to all four language modes on a recursive and developmental pattern. Ability in English is a broad and complex area and we need to ensure that we retain a curriculum and an assessment system that is sufficiently flexible and open. The following chapters provide a thorough examination of the best ways of supporting and developing pupils in English of all abilities.

CHAPTER 2

Defining high ability in English

What does it mean to be 'good at English'?

In the Introduction (Chapter 1) I discussed how English as a school subject is seen by all interested parties as pre-eminent amongst school subjects yet it has never been defined neatly to anyone's entire satisfaction. This rather paradoxical position means that the consensus about the value of English must be set against the proliferation of oppositional views about the content and purpose of the subject. A problem of these proportions helps to explain why what being 'good at English' actually *means* is almost nowhere to be found. Some recent attempts such as the levels of the National Curriculum have been notoriously unsuccessful in helping teachers to assess pupils' progress in English. GCSE grade criteria were certainly more successful and were relatively well received by the profession. The National Curriculum is developing level descriptions which seem potentially more useful but there are adverse reactions to this idea, pointing out the inadequacy of such an approach for a subject which involves a complex interaction between the four language modes.

An examination of the literature does not take us much further. If you examine a great many books on English teaching you will find numerous references to ability but you will rarely find the term itself defined or even mentioned in the index. I have tried in Chapter 1 to explain why ability is largely missing from discussions of the subject or even from books that centre on assessment in English. There is a very comprehensive literature (Young and Tyre 1992) dealing with gifted children but I am concerned with the significant proportion of pupils who might be considered 'very good', rather than a tiny percentage who are defined as being off the end of any normal scale.

My approach is to try to develop a useful description of the very able in English and so part of that approach involves looking at some pupils picked out by their English teachers as 'outstanding'. By analysing their characteristics it may be possible to develop a model of what 'being good at English' might mean and, therefore, what it means to be exceptionally able at English. This idea is explored in one aspect of some research, described in detail below, that suggests that there are clusters of characteristics, identified by teachers and pupils, that provide us with some useful pointers about ability in English. It is also useful to know that there is largely a match between what pupils think being good at English means and what their teachers currently identify.

Although there seems to be a valuable match between pupil and teacher perceptions, teachers themselves are somewhat at a loss when it comes to providing for the most able. For example, many teachers interviewed in the study felt very ill at ease with any strict definition of ability in English and they also expressed considerable uncertainty about what to do with very able pupils; they felt that they could recognise them as individuals but were unclear how to help them. As one experienced teacher put it when asked what should be done for the most able in English, 'I wish I knew.' This is initially surprising in a subject which has consistently valued mixed ability teaching with a strong emphasis on intimate teacher knowledge of individuals (Mills 1987). However, the most commonly cited strategy in English is differentiation by outcome; that is, where a common task can be attempted by different abilities producing a range of levels of achievement. This approach, whilst perfectly effective in itself, does not acknowledge the point that the most able may have different needs, some of which might be defined as special.

The Introductory Chapter considered why the majority of English teachers are mostly concerned with development and personal growth (Goodwyn 1992); hence ability, in any abstract sense, is simply not a major issue for them. However, there is a powerful wish within English teachers to ensure that personal growth, whilst essentially an anti-elitist view, is not about levelling down to some vague notion of the average achiever. The crucial point is that all pupils should be moving forward and that it is seen as inevitable that their progress will be uneven and perhaps better viewed as occurring in fits and starts than in any smooth form of progression.

It is also well established that there is a strong correlation between maturation and capability in English. Certain kinds of response, to literature in particular, which are used by teachers and examiners as markers of progress and/or achievement seem only possible when individuals have arrived at a degree of emotional maturity (Protherough 1986). Such a view of ability in the subject contrasts strongly with views in mathematics, science or music. A number of teachers in this study commented on this maturational factor in general and as at least partially accounting for gender differences; they felt that boys' relative immaturity in Key Stage 3 kept them behind but that they caught up and, in the view of a few teachers, forged ahead at 'A' level. However, when picking out their able pupils, high ability was found in an almost equal distribution across the sexes. The way younger, high ability boys were described, suggests that part of their early success is due to their unusual maturity for their age.

Given the lack of teacher and school-centred research about ability in English it seemed important to examine current opinions and perceptions in schools and to attempt to formulate a model of ability in school based on actual practice.

The Research Study

The study itself was undertaken in three contrasting schools in the summer term of 1993. The schools were selected on the basis of their differences from each other and their close links with their local University (Reading). School A is a selective girls' grammar school drawing pupils from an entire county; School B an urban, mixed 11–18 comprehensive from a dense area of housing; and School C a rural/suburban mixed 11–18 comprehensive. Another school, a boys' grammar, was included in the original research plan but withdrew because of various pressures on its teachers.

School A is in many ways a traditional academic school with some of the best examination results in the country. English is a very popular subject in the Sixth Form and in the school generally. School B has a very mixed catchment area, partly private and partly council housing, and examination results are modest. English is a popular subject in the school and there is a small 'A' level group in the small Sixth Form. School C is an unusually large comprehensive school in a predominantly affluent area and has a very large Sixth Form in which English is strongly represented.

Each school was approached and agreed to take part on the basis of an interest in the project. The study involved interviewing members of each English Department and a range of pupils from each year and the completion of questionnaires by a sample of classes. The underlying question for all participants was what does being good at English mean to you?

The teachers

The teachers, eighteen in all, were interviewed individually and first asked to provide a brief autobiographical sketch of their careers and then to describe at least one of their pupils who they felt was outstandingly good at English. All interviews were recorded. After some detailed discussion of this pupil they were asked to comment on what they felt more generally about English and ability, to speculate on any gender differences in ability, to describe how they identified and then taught very able pupils and finally to comment on the value of the National Curriculum in relation to able pupils. It is worth stating immediately that all the teachers welcomed the framework of the National Curriculum and every individual rejected the levels as at best distracting and at worst as completely distorting. Each tape was transcribed and analysed for key words and phrases.

The teachers provided a variety of views but there was no distinctive difference between departments or schools. Looking at the general question about being good at English first, the following characteristics emerged. Two thirds mentioned technical skills of some kind with special emphasis on the first phase of secondary school. This suggests that English teachers definitely associate a mastery of spelling, punctuation and correctness with being good at English. Critics of the profession might take note of this simple and rather predictable finding. Writing and reading received the most specific comments. Good pupils are fluent writers with control over content and form, and an awareness of the need to plan and structure work. There will be touches of flair and originality in their writing, and evidence of imagination and creativity in the work. Such pupils also read a good deal although quantity is more important than other factors. Teachers stress that successful pupils will tend to have an immediate understanding of what they read but with a willingness to reread and so develop a clearer personal response to a text. These pupils tend to be confident and articulate speakers although there is a problem with some over 'reticence' or 'being quiet'. In the interviews there was a sprinkling of references to enthusiasm, sensitivity, enjoyment and so on but it was clear from the transcripts that most pupils could be good at English without it being their main enthusiasm. Many able pupils selected by their teachers to be interviewed as part of the project had several other subjects that they preferred to English.

The interviewees had no trouble in picking out their very able pupils and there is a remarkable unanimity in the comments made about the distinctive features of the very able in English. Whether talking about a Year 7 or a Year 11 pupil, two thirds of the sample commented on or discussed in detail the notion of a maturity well beyond the chronological age and this maturity is evident across all four language modes. The next most important factor and often linked with it in discussion was depth and

18

breadth of reading. Such pupils not only read widely but they read 'adult' and 'complex' texts and they are constantly looking for more and more challenging material. Some such pupils are gifted in reading out loud but the truly distinctive feature is in response to literature and this responsiveness is mainly expressed in written form revealing depth of analysis as well as feeling. Several teachers made it clear that they felt what might be called omnivorous reading was a good factor in developing pupils in English but they also suggested that to be an outstanding pupil then challenging material had to be included. In School A (the most traditionally academic in a historic sense) this was the single most identifiable feature of a very able pupil. Strategies offered to help the able will be discussed later but the most common action involved recommending books to these exceptional readers.

The most consistently used descriptive domain was to do with imagination and this word predominates in relation to the very able pupil; other terms like creativity, flair, good ideas and originality seem to come within this domain. All these words were in a sense taken for granted, there was no attempt to explain what they meant in relation to pupils; the implication was that all pupils have these qualities to some extent but the exceptionally able stand out through displaying them consistently, especially in their writing. In this way teachers seem to foreground the creative artist as the key model. Several teachers commented on how much they looked forward to reading and to responding to the pupil's work. This point connects very clearly with my discussion in Chapter 1 about the influential notions of the original artist.

All the teachers discussed speaking and listening and twelve of the pupils described were very articulate and confident. They were also characterised as good contributors, sometimes as exceptionally good listeners and six of this group were good at leading group discussions and this latter point connects interestingly with the only strategy suggested for the most able within the spoken language mode (see below). The other six pupils were all considered quiet or reticent and each teacher was unsure how capable they might be orally. In this category one girl was mentioned as shy and even introverted but 'a remarkably good actress'. Three others from the confident group were commented on as good at drama work and two of those were involved in drama outside the school. This emphasis on the dramatic suggests that English teachers see a performance element within high ability.

Overall, the fact that most of the chosen pupils were interactive and confident rather disrupts the mythology of the quiet, isolated, suffering artist whose originality is misunderstood by the rest of the class. Notably only one of the pupils, a boy in Year 10, was described as at all difficult and this was by reputation in other subjects where 'he is easily bored and becomes very awkward' but this 'has not happened in English yet'. The characteristic of being bored and causing trouble has often been mentioned as a feature of the most able but it is curiously absent from this small sample. However, it is noticeable that ten of the eighteen pupils came from Years 7 and 8, so early enthusiasm for secondary school is clearly a potential factor. The other, older pupils, including the boy mentioned above, did not cause visible problems because of their exceptional ability.

This apparent conformity exists alongside numerous comments on how such pupils are often highly independent and self-motivating. In a sense these pupils are always working on English because they are serious readers; this is an element in what sets them apart and is viewed as evidence of their comparative maturity but, more significantly, as partly explaining it.

The characteristics outlined above have some variation according to gender. All these able pupils are distinguished by imagination and creativity but two boys are picked out for their self-reliance and systematic approach to their work. Another boy is considered 'not to read as much as I would like'. There is an underlying sense that able boys and girls are rather different in the way they approach their work and the implication is that they may need rather different support if they are to be stretched.

Overall, two views emerged about gender and ability. The majority view is that there is no essential difference in ability. The difference is in attitude. Girls were seen as more mature than boys, especially in Years 7 to 9. This maturity is revealed not only in the quality of their writing and talking but also in their conscientiousness and thoroughness. Girls are seen as far more at ease with their achievements in English, they are open about their emotional reactions to reading and the fact that they read far more widely then most boys gives them an 'extra dimension of experience'. Girls are 'less inhibited about wanting to do well', 'they don't mind being good', whereas boys are 'more subject to peer pressure', 'more prone to primary school behaviour' and 'want to be funny all the time'.

In this view boys eventually catch up, usually in Key Stage 4 – 'they are more motivated by the idea of a course'. At 'A' level, according to one highly experienced 'A' level examiner in the sample, they overtake the majority of girls. She described how she felt that girls lacked distance from texts and allowed their emotional responses to dominate them, whilst boys became much clearer and more analytical in their thinking and writing, 'perhaps empathy and sensitivity are more feminine characteristics?'. She commented that boys could say much more with fewer words. The idea that boys become more adept at controlling their emotional reactions is well understood. It is a topic worthy of further study to examine at what cost and with what attendant loss they manage this control.

The second, minority view, is that girls simply do have more aptitude for English and that this aptitude is enhanced by their better attitude to work and also by the fact that 'Although this view is changing, English is still seen as a sissy subject', 'girls are more in tune with English' and 'boys are not expected to be interested in English'. The idea that English is perceived as a feminine subject has a long history. Examination and 11–plus results would suggest that superior female achievement in English is absolute. This research study, small though it is in scale, suggests a clear conviction amongst English teachers that the most able in the subject includes equal proportions of boys and girls and that differences are not to do with ability but with a marked difference in attitude. Boys' underachievement remains the key issue. This view is heavily endorsed by the pupils themselves.

The pupils

Pupils were interviewed in a variety of ways, some on their own with one researcher, some in small groups with one or two researchers and some in pairs with one researcher. The children were selected by their teachers as representing high, medium and lower levels of ability, and pupils were chosen from each year group. All interviews were recorded. Pupils were first asked something about their interests outside school and in school and then where they placed English in their hierarchy of favourite subjects. They were then asked to pick out someone in their English class who they felt was good and describe what that pupil was like. They were then asked to compare themselves to that pupil and then to comment on what being good in English involved. They were asked to describe what they thought English teachers were looking for and also on the extent of praise given by such teachers. Their views on gender differences were sought and then, finally, whether they would change anything about English if they could.

Even pupils in School A, the girls' grammar, do not provide a simple unified view of what being good at English means; however, they can be usefully grouped in the following ways. Pupils in Key Stage 3, whatever their ability, put a great deal of stress on technical proficiency, e.g. spelling, punctuation, grammar and handwriting; without these characteristics, the pupils felt, you could not be considered good at English. You also had to write good stories, be good at speaking out in class discussion and for some be good in drama. Reading is important, especially reading widely and being good 'out loud'. The 'less' able pupils put most emphasis on technical proficiency in writing and tended to stress confidence in speaking but in contrast to their own lack of confidence and success as contributors in English or drama.

Pupils in Key Stage 4 continued to mention technical proficiency but with far less emphasis. To them being good at English involved a whole range of possibilities. They all stressed reading, especially private reading. The most able pupils found work on set books very tedious and rather plodding; as one pupil put it, 'it's all so obvious' – she preferred her own books, was currently more interested in philosophy and especially enjoyed Marx and Foucault! A great many pupils stressed how dull they found it to 'plod through books'.

Pupils in the two mixed schools had broadly similar views to those expressed above. They placed exactly the same emphasis in Key Stage 3 on technical matters with more emphasis at Key Stage 4 on reading and on being creative.

All the pupils in the interviews had a view about gender and ability. They were unanimous in considering that girls work harder and pay much better attention in English lessons. There was a slight majority, evenly distributed across the sexes, who felt that girls were actually more able than boys. They considered girls more responsive to books, more imaginative and better at absorbing ideas from others. Those who felt there was no difference stressed that English provided equal opportunities for both sexes to do well.

The surveys

Over 700 pupils were surveyed for the study, representing Years 7, 8, 9 and 10 in each school, with a few sixth formers also participating. Because one school was a girls' school the sample contains about 65% of female responses and this has been taken into account when analysing the data. Two different kinds of survey were used in order to provide some cross-checking of results.

Survey A encouraged pupils to respond as openly as possible. The questionnaire began, 'We are trying to find out what pupils in school think about English and, in particular, what you think it takes to be *good* at English. Using as much detail as you can, put down exactly what you think, there is no right opinion, we simply want your genuine opinion. These questions are just to help you think. What makes some people good at English? Think of the people you know who are good at English and jot down what they are like. You might find it helpful to think about:

– their reading
– their writing
– their speaking and listening.

Feel free to discuss your opinions with others in your class but make sure that what you write down is what *you* think.'

Initially a random sample of the pupil responses from both question-naires was analysed and a range of categories was developed and then applied to the complete survey.

The model of ability that emerges is chiefly shared by both sexes. In the writing mode, spelling receives the most mentions and is closely followed by neat presentation and good handwriting. It is also seen as crucial to punctuate accurately and to develop a wide vocabulary. Being 'Imaginative' comes next to spelling but if this category is blended with 'Creative' and 'Original' then this category overtakes spelling. In reading, the most cited category is wide reading and this category is the most pop-ular of all. Being a fluent, expressive reader is highly valued but under-standing and comprehension are seen as less important. In speaking, con-fidence and expression are seen as vital but being a good listener is rated highest of all. There are a few references to liking English or having a good teacher but these are so few as to suggest that this is not a major concern for pupils. This view is partly confirmed by the fact that good behaviour and concentration are seen as very important in order to do well in English – this point is always more likely to be expressed by a boy.

Survey B very much supports these main points. It was a deliberately 'closed' survey, asking for specific answers and for pupils to select choices from a limited range. The survey was headed, 'We are trying to find out what pupils in school think about English and, in particular, what you think being *good* at English actually means. Could you please answer all the questions and put down exactly what you think; there is no right answer, we simply want your real opinion'. The questions were:

- Think of someone you know in your year who is good at English. Write down what makes him or her especially good.
- How many people in your class would you say are very good at English?
- What kinds of things do teachers say about pupils who are good at English?
- How can a teacher tell if someone is very good at English?
- In general are girls better at English than boys; please explain your opinion.

Spelling again receives the most emphasis and is accompanied by good presentation and also by accurate punctuation. Having a wide vocabulary comes out slightly more strongly in these responses as does being a fluent and expressive writer. 'Imaginative' is the second greatest category but if mixed in with 'Creative' and 'Original' then it becomes easily the largest with far more mentions than any other term. Notably the word 'original' is hardly used by any of the pupils, only fifteen direct mentions from the whole survey. This does not mean that pupils do not understand originality as a concept but it clearly shows that creativity and, most of all, being imaginative are seen as the real evidence of being good at English. In reading, and speaking and listening, the pupils' responses mirror exactly the points from Survey A.

As a part of Survey B, pupils were asked to rank a series of terms by ringing the ones that they felt best describe people who are good at English. They were asked to think about what being good at English means to them. The terms are:

- Imaginative
- Creative
- Good with facts
- Reads aloud well
- Reads lots of books
- Reads good books
- Good speller
- Writes good stories
- Neat handwriting
- Explains ideas clearly
- Tells good stories
- Listens well to others
- Watches lots of TV
- Watches lots of films.

Pupils could rank these as Very Important, Important, Not Important and Completely Unimportant.

Their responses confirm the findings of Survey A and they add some extra insights into pupils' perceptions. The basic points about being creative and imaginative are firmly endorsed, they have the second and third highest scores respectively. The highest score of all is given to 'Explains ideas clearly', whereas 'Tells good stories' gains only a medium score. This score, combined with pupil comments elsewhere, suggests that this more intellectual mode of talk is considered a real characteristic of ability in English. It is echoed above by the teachers' strategy for the most able of giving them important and often 'leadership' roles in group work. 'Listens well to others' receives a very high score and shows how aware pupils are of the interactive nature of speaking and listening.

Although spelling receives a high score and it is sixth overall, it comes behind 'Writes good stories' and 10% actually rated spelling as 'Completely Unimportant', the great majority of that group coming from the grammar school. Girls from that school were also the majority group in the 35% who rated 'Neat handwriting' as 'Completely Unimportant'. This finding suggests that in that school context some of the mechanics of the language become much less important in the pupils' eyes, presumably because they are expected to have reached a high level already and, in a literal sense, because the pupils themselves would not be there if they had not already demonstrated their proficiency.

Reading emerges with a slightly different emphasis in these responses. In the two surveys, wide reading was the key and here (Survey B) it is highly rated but nearly 20% thought it was not important. Boys especially indicate a lower value for wide reading. 'Reads aloud well' is considered not important by 35% of pupils and nearly 45% did not consider that 'Reads good books' was necessary to be good at the subject. This view also fits with teachers' views that a wide, eclectic range is the best for development.

The final two categories on watching television and films produced very low scores – only about 15% in each section thought this helped with English. The term 'lots' may have had something to do with this reaction. My interpretation of the evidence from this particular set of responses and from pupil interviews and comments is that children do not think of media-related work in English as at all connected to their own leisure viewing, whereas there is a suggestion in the reading response on 'Reads good books' that a broad view of reading is seen as conducive to success in English. This suggests that pupils still operate a relatively traditional model of English in which books are the principal content and clearly the evidence of this study is that teachers do as well.

As part of Survey B pupils were asked about gender and ability in English. They were asked whether girls or boys are better at English or whether there is no difference and to provide any reasons to support their views. The figures here speak for themselves: 166 pupils thought girls are better, 43 were boys and 123 were girls. Only fifteen pupils thought boys are better, eleven boys (ten from the same school) and four girls. There were 162 in the no difference category, 74 male and 88 female but a considerable proportion, about half, felt that girls did achieve more. There were eight abstentions and fifteen 'did not knows', all from the girls' school. The girls' school returns also contained a considerable number of comments about this being a 'sexist question'. On this basis the majority of pupils consider that girls' have more ability and the overwhelming majority consider that girls make much of their ability.

The reasons fall into some interesting categories. Throughout the responses there is almost an obsession from both genders with boys' behaviour. The key words, whether commenting on ability or achievement, are attention and concentration; about 80% of respondents comment negatively on boys and positively on girls in this respect. Linked to these key words are terms like behaviour, patience and maturity. Comments from both sexes focus on boys' inability to work in groups, their constant attempts to distract each other and their need to attract attention. These observations correlate neatly with teachers' views on the most able boys whose maturity sets them apart from their peers.

The majority of girls also offered some discrete reasons for girls having more ability and these have interesting implications for their perception of what English is all about. About 60% of girls who felt girls were better, commented on the fact they they are more able to deal with feelings and emotions and could express these in both talk and writing. About 50% commented on girls being highly imaginative. A small number of girls made observations about boys' interests, 'boys only think about football', 'boys don't think much', 'boys have more interest in facts', 'they have more mathematical minds' and 'they only want to talk about sport and computers'. Almost all the boys who felt that girls were more able put this down to a greater ability to concentrate, more interest in books and more interest in the subject. About a third of boys in this category thought that there were more female teachers and that they favoured girls over boys. It seems that both girls and boys do see English as more of a female domain.

The respondents who felt that there was no real difference between boys and girls still thought that girls achieved more but a combination of 'natural' ability and hard work would bring success in English.

Some conclusions

There is a striking correlation between all these findings, suggesting that it is very possible to construct a model of ability in English, based on actual classroom practice. It is also evident that the model is a literary one although it has a small and not a large letter 'l'. English teachers relate high ability to serious readers but they see quantities of reading as more valuable than any simplistic notion of good 'texts'. This emphasis would seem to fit with their own experience as readers: English teachers tend to have been omnivorous readers themselves until their degree courses (Goodwyn 1993).

It seems then that being good at English is very much about reading but it does seem significant that this is not a canonical notion, it is much more of a Cultural Analysis than a Cultural Heritage model (see Chapter 1). The outstanding quality is being imaginative, valued by teachers and pupils above everything else. This quality is demonstrated principally through writing and so we see again how the literary model dominates;

successful readers of imaginative writing become successful producers of imaginative writing.

In the writing mode, despite this overarching emphasis on the imaginative, technical matters dominate. Almost all the pupils in the survey perceived spelling as an absolute prerequisite of being good at English, the unanimity of this finding is very striking.

In speaking and listening there are some unsurprising views about being confident and articulate but a more important finding is that being a good listener is valued most highly; this point is particularly emphasised when teachers and pupils are considering the most able in the subject. It is also clear that teachers in particular relate group leadership to ability in English. This becomes an interesting finding when set alongside the consistent stress on being a good listener; it does not suggest a model of dominant leadership but rather one based on a notion of the facilitator.

The most able in English are picked out for having that facilitative quality in particular. They are not seen as antisocial or isolated figures but as interactive and contributing. They are especially marked by their ability to read widely and to respond to literature imaginatively, often in writing. It seems from the research described above that there are many pupils who fall into this category and so, although they may have very real needs, they are not in a tiny, 'special' minority.

It is initially somewhat surprising, given English teachers' knowledge of individual pupils, that they do not appear to be confident about supporting the most able. However, I would suggest that this diffidence comes from two sources. The first source is the model of Personal Growth. This model is not competitive, it places fundamental importance on the development of the individual as an individual, not in relation to others. The second source is the idea of differentiation by outcome. This idea is fine as far as it goes, there are many written assignments in particular that lend themselves to genuine differentiation by outcome. However, differentiation cannot be simply equated with appropriateness. The most able in English appear to need certain kinds of support that might enable them to develop at a pace that suits them better. One has only to recall the pupil (see above) who mentioned that most work on texts was all so obvious, to remember that differentiation will need, at times, to be by input as well as outcome. However, this notion of differentiation is not to be confused with setting. English teachers generally consider a mixture of abilities to be a positive advantage to all pupils.

Finally a few pointers emerge for supporting the most able in English. The following suggestions for helping the most able are based on the research outlined above.

The most able can be male or female and can be identified by their noticeable maturity beyond their years. They tend to enjoy challenging texts but they are more interested in wide reading than in a few canonical texts. They have immediate responses to their reading but are marked by a wish to return to those responses and to re-evaluate them. They write in very imaginative ways and are technically proficient. They are usually articulate and confident speakers but are more marked by their ability to listen well and to explain for the benefit of others. This facility is especially evident in group work where they can take on powerful but not dominating leadership roles.

English teachers can adopt some or all of the following approaches with these individuals:

– Keeping track of their reading and providing a constant source of suggestions – these would be both for challenging texts and also simply for range.
– Providing brief tutorial type sessions to discuss reading progress.
– Providing specific reading tasks that require initial and then deeper and more evaluative responses.
– Setting writing tasks that make the most of pupils' imaginative potential.
– Placing pupils in leadership roles in group situations.
– Providing oral tasks that require pupils to analyse and explain.

These approaches are perfectly suitable for any pupil and what they require for the most able is more emphasis, more tracking by the teacher and more willingness to intervene rather than letting these pupils just get on by themselves.

CHAPTER 3

Mixed ability

Introduction

At the end of a secondary Heads of English meeting about National Curriculum assessment, I overheard two colleagues discussing the issue of mixed ability. 'We're phasing out mixed ability from Year 9,' said one, 'with Years 7 and 8 under review for the following year.' The other nodded agreement, 'There's no way we can justify it, given the present testing arrangements. Sadly, it will have to go.' As a teacher trained in the ideological white-heat of the 1970s, this sounded to me an almost sacrilegious utterance. I entered the discussion with indignant relish, challenging their apparent acquiescence and reactiveness to educational policies, and rather archly reminding them of their 'principles'. 'What is the case for mixed ability anyway?' one of them replied. 'If there ever was a sound educational case, most of us have long forgotten it.'

The use of mixed ability teaching in English has become a neglected issue. Once the subject of impassioned debate and a catch-all slogan for a radical, new paradigm of teaching in the seventies, the mixed ability philosophy has become naturalised into routine practice. The arguments for it have long been assimilated by English teachers; generations of students have survived it. There have always been reservations expressed by certain English teachers about the operation of mixed ability teaching: its perceived failure to 'stretch' the more able or to address the specific learning difficulties of the least able; its demands upon teacher time, expertise and upon departmental resources; the difficulties it poses for differentiating students' work for assessment purposes, and so on. But during the 1980s, departments tended to weather or to resolve these problems with varying degrees of success, and mixed ability prevailed as the most common means of grouping students (particularly in the lower years) of secondary school English. Yet despite its continued popularity, my own investigations show simply that mixed ability has gradually ceased to be an interesting issue: the implications of teaching it effectively are rarely considered on conferences or courses, and a periodical and literature search has revealed that research writing on it is both scanty and uninspiring.

Indeed, my research shows that recent developments in education have precipitated a gradual erosion in the use of mixed ability in English, particularly in the upper school. The introduction of a National Curriculum in English in March 1990 has a model of assessment which was predicated on the notion that students could be assigned to hierarchical levels of competence and achievement in each of the four language modes. This model was further reinforced by the introduction of tiers of entry at certain Key Stages, which would be assessed by Standard Attainment Tests (SATs). This has placed various pressures on Heads of English who were responsible for preparing cohorts of students for a wide range of assessment levels. For many in the sample group interviewed, the pressure has proved too much and they were resorting, often as a 'quick fix' solution, to some form of selective grouping from Year 9 upwards. Why should mixed ability bother us now? Should we accept that it is a spent force? Or is there a fresh case to be made for revitalising the debate on the ways in which we group our students through secondary school? My research reveals that English Departments are once again questioning from first principles the way they group students; that feelings on the issue are just as passionately held and just as strongly expressed as they were in the seventies. The difference lies in the collective repository of experience which now informs the views of English teachers, and in their awareness of the particular social and economic future which faces the children they teach.

This chapter draws upon a small-scale research project I carried out during 1993 into the significance of mixed ability English teaching for the l990s. I decided to investigate the views of a range of English teachers, using a questionnaire, a series of in-depth interviews with individual teachers, and departmental discussion groups. I also drew upon the research work of Vanessa Culver[1] into pupil attitudes towards mixed ability and selective groupings. My findings are not presented as conclusive or definitive; rather they aim to clarify the parameters of the new debate on mixed ability. They provide a pluralistic range of 'voices' and viewpoints: diverse, eclectic, sometimes tentative or contradictory but always convinced that there are educational principles at stake.

[1] Vanessa Culver was a PGCE student at the University of Reading from 1992–3 when she carried out research into pupils' attitudes to mixed ability and streamed groupings. Her findings were written up in an unpublished coursework essay.

What is mixed ability?

The starting point of my research was to investigate whether English teachers share a common set of understandings of 'mixed ability'. This phrase has become so familiar through excessive exposure that it is easy to assume a shared interpretation. It is a popular umbrella term which is frequently used synonymously with heterogeneous, unstreamed, non-streamed, 'natural' or unselected groups. In 1981, an NFER survey (NFER 1981) into the role of mixed ability teaching found that it covered a wide variety of organisations and procedures in very different school environments. To what extent have these meanings evolved into a shared working definition in the 1990s? How have the changing educational and ideological contexts informed that definition? It is probably true to say that there has always been a confusion about, if not a suspicion of the term. Educationally, consensus on what constitutes 'ability' has consistently eluded social scientists and teachers. This is exemplified in early definitions of mixed ability, such as that given in the report of an ILEA inspectorate survey on mixed ability grouping in 1976:

> …in its purest form this type of organisation groups pupils in such a way that each class in the year group is assumed to have an *equal range of attainment*. Each class remains together for all subjects, except where separately grouped by subjects (as in physical education) or divided into sub-groups (as in craft work). (ILEA 1976.)

This definition reveals a dominant reading of the phrase 'mixed ability'. First there is the connotation that the selection of mixed ability classes is a 'natural' process, which has somehow mirrored the range of ability and attainment in the population at large. This is based on a prevailing myth that, in contrast to a streamed class, a typical mixed ability Year 7 class is randomly or arbitrarily selected. Gregory exemplified this when he wrote that, 'No pupil assessment or knowledge of the pupils' abilities or skills is required in order to set up mixed-ability groups, whereas streaming and setting done properly requires detailed knowledge of the pupils' attainments.' (Gregory 1986). Interestingly, this same belief is also revealed in my interviews with English teachers. A typical definition of mixed ability was, 'That in one class you have a total range of ability from the most able to the least able pupils with *no obvious selection having taken place first,* (my italics) except in terms of which children work best together.'[2]

---

[2] All quotations from English teachers in this chapter are selected from a series of interviews I conducted with staff at the following schools in 1993: Robert May's School, Odiham, Hampshire; Newlands School, Maidenhead, Berks; The Kennet School, Thatcham, Berks. All quotations from teachers are unattributed in order to preserve anonymity. No further references will be made to the source of the quotation from teachers interviewed.

Second, the ILEA statement makes the assumption that ability is synonymous with aspects of attainment. This is part of a reading of 'mixed ability' which has traditionally and persistently confused the relationship between ability and achievement – a relationship affected by such factors as motivation, attitudes and specific skills. In 1976, Adelman criticised the unreliable basis upon which many mixed ability classes were selected:

> By what criteria, tests and reports is a mixed ability class constituted? There is no consistency of selection across secondary schools. I suspect that generally pupils are selected not by their ability but on their school achievements; on the basis of success by the criteria and standards of the school rather than a standard psychometric test of intellectual potential. 'Ability' may be assessed by psychometric tests. Achievement is bound up with the social context of teaching and learning. The docile and obedient – the rule-learning, are mixed with a population of 'hard cases' – a 'mixed ability' bunch of resistors to the social order of the school. (Adelman 1976.)

Adelman's point that mixed ability grouping by attainment was often a thin disguise for a system of social and behavioural control was taken up by an HMI report on mixed ability in 1978: 'Mixed ability organisation was very often adopted as a means to the solution of urgent problems – largely of discipline, morale or motivation – seen as arising from the organisation of classes by ability.' (HMI 1978.) This use of mixed ability grouping by some schools, without any apparent educational rationale, may be part of the reason why 'mixed ability' has had a less sympathetic press in recent years, when the political climate has become more hostile to the ideals of comprehensive schooling. As Helen Moriarty pointed out in 1987:

> For parents, mixed attitude is likely to be far more alarming than mixed ability. It's not the less able kids who worry the parents of bright ones; it's the obstructive or destructive ones who threaten good order and progress. (Moriarty 1987.)

So if 'mixed ability' has become a catch-all phrase for any class of children who have not been selected by academic criteria, does it still retain credibility for today's teachers? My research shows that it can do, because what is emerging is a more sophisticated reading of the phrase and the principles which construct it. This reading has developed from the richer understanding English teachers in particular have formed of the nature of ability within English. A fuller discussion of this is developed throughout the book (see Chapters 1 and 2), but my research of teachers' views found that they shared many of the following assumptions.

- 'Ability' in English is a very difficult concept to categorise.
- Personal qualities of engagement, flexibility, imagination, social skills, open-mindedness, motivation, conviction are just as important as intellectual qualities such as criticality, reading skills, ability to communicate and so on: such qualities are almost impossible to 'measure'.
- The range of ability within the four language modes in any one student is unpredictably diverse – for example, a student labelled less able in her writing can often be very able in oral work.
- Ability in English is 'one of those subjects we can all do and all know that we can do, and that creates a particular set of presumptions and preconceptions which children bring to the classroom with them. There is a level of competence there which other subjects don't have.'
- Learning in English is a spiral, recursive and accumulative process, not a linear, sequential, hierarchical one.

From this set of statements follow two central implications for English teachers. The first is that, in one sense, all groups, even the most rigorously streamed, contain a range of ability and also a range of attainments. It is then the width of the range which is the central issue: a mixed ability class contains a wider range of whatever is meant by 'ability' than a selective class.

The second implication is that English as a subject seems an ideal environment for the mixed ability principle to flourish. The very diversity of ability in a class is central to the enrichment of a student's educational experience. This does not imply however that any random selection of students will do; nor necessarily that primary school attainments records, which often determine the composition of Year 7 registration groups and therefore teaching groups, should be the leading criterion for selecting mixed ability groups. Rather this view that English is a perfect 'home' for mixed ability suggests that careful selection of students is paramount – to ensure that a genuine 'mix' of individuals in a group is accomplished. Indeed one Head of English described the business of creating 'genuine' mixed ability groups as a 'three or four week process at any year level.' Far from being random, a number of vital factors must be considered:

> It means creating groups that are organised in such a way that the range, the spread of ability, background, gender, need and attainment is as wide as possible across the year group...that's probably a far more sophisticated and complex process than streaming or setting allows.

Given the complexity of this process, to justify teachers using mixed ability, it is necessary to examine the case more closely.

What is the case for mixed ability?

A brief review of the literature on mixed ability grouping in the 1970s reveals the fundamental ideological and educational arguments at the heart of the case. Bailey and Bridges, in their study of the reasons why teachers appeared to support mixed ability grouping identified a series of commonly held principles:

- justice or equality of opportunity;
- equality of respect (or value) for individuals;
- fraternity – living within an integrated, mutually supportive, interactive community. (Bailey and Bridges 1983.)

These principles pointed to a notion of an ideal society, which mixed ability groupings within a comprehensive school setting might hope both to reflect and eventually to contribute to.

> The ideal society on this view is a community (a commune?) which is at least relatively unhierarchical in character; in which there is a mutuality of concern and respect, and co-operation in the pursuit of collective and common good; in which there is a willing acceptance of the principle that no individual or group interest will persistently be subordinated to another – for all of which a certain kind of equality of consideration will be necessary. (Bailey and Bridges 1983.)

It was this notion of creating an egalitarian society without class divisions which seventies research revealed were being actively encouraged by mixed ability practices in schools. The Banbury experiment exemplified this, where a large school with four separate 'halls' of students proved eminently researchable because two went mixed ability and two continued with streaming. The Banbury Inquiry found that although there was little evident difference between the academic achievements of the children monitored, there were definite social advantages:

> There is evidence that children tend to associate with others of their own ability, but this is significantly and markedly less in the mixed ability forms than in the streamed forms. Not only is there more opportunity for children of differing abilities to meet more easily when they are based on mixed ability forms, it actually happens that they take advantage of it at all ability levels. (Newbold 1977.)

The 1981 NFER survey, explains that the initiative to 'go mixed ability' in the late-1970s was taken in most cases by Heads who cited *ideological*, rather than educational or practical reasons for their decisions. 'Unstreaming is socially undesirable; you shouldn't have all the kids with dirty vests in one form.' From the head of a former grammar school confronted with the first comprehensive intake: 'The acquisition of knowledge is not the be-all and end-all of education. Basically, the decision to unstream was social and not academic.'

So if an ideological preference for the social effects of mixed ability were instrumental in guiding school and departmental policies for grouping students in the seventies, is this still a significant factor today? My interviews with English teachers in comprehensive schools suggest that this broadly socialist rationale for mixed ability teaching is residual – almost a forgotten memory. There was a wistful, rather nostalgic longing for a lost past in the comment of one teacher:

'I would prefer to be contributing towards a society that shares and interacts in a co-operative fashion, which seems to me to be fundamental features of the good mixed ability classroom, rather than to a society that is confrontational and competitive, which is the ideological underpinning of streaming.'

But for most of those teachers who continue to support mixed ability, the case is still passionately made, but significantly is now founded on lengthy and diverse experience: they cite explicitly **educational** rather than socio-ideological reasons for their case, drawing upon a range of examples from different moments in their teaching histories. While many of their reasons echo arguments from the past, there is a strong sense that a metamorphosed version of mixed ability is emerging for the decade, which may be resilient enough to withstand attacks upon it from politicians and educationalists[3], and convince teachers who may doubt its value and relevance. Today's case for mixed ability can be distilled down to three central principles:

(i) The educational value of mixing ability levels

The first principle is *the mixing of ability levels* – the benefits mixed ability teaching confers to children of differing levels of ability. In my survey[4], 81% of English teachers interviewed felt that mixed ability groups offered a positive and rewarding environment for 'less able' pupils; 78% of teachers felt that this was true for pupils in the 'middle' range, and 57% of teachers felt this was true for the 'more able' pupils. This sense that mixed ability is generally good for all levels of ability was amplified by one teacher:

'If you group by ability, you simply reinforce expectations of what pupils can do at a particular level. Mixed ability frees [them] from the feeling that they have been stereotyped according to a given ability. It liberates them to do better.'

---

[3] Channel 4 Commission on Education (1991), *Every Child in Britain*, Granada TV. A wave of support for overtly selective methods of grouping pupils was expressed publicly by a group of politicians and educationalists.

[4] I conducted a survey by questionnaire of 42 secondary English teachers in 1993 to learn something of teachers' attitudes towards the use of mixed ability and selective groupings in English.

The strong support shown for the advantages to the 'less able' of mixed ability has been a consistent and well documented feature of its history. The knowledge that being a member of a mixed ability group had a **motivational** value for 'less' able pupils, was behind the change from selective to mixed ability groupings in the 1970s. Teachers today still recognise the close link between behaviour, motivation and attainment as critical for an effective learning environment at all levels of ability:

'Once everyone is working [in a mixed ability class], they want to be part of the majority; when everyone else is working, the expectation is that they will work.'

Now, teachers also emphasise the **educational** significance of the mixed ability class as a learning environment:

'[Mixed ability] gives less able pupils a much better chance...they're able to widen their views and their experience because of the input of ideas from the more able children.'

For those pupils of broadly average ability, it was interesting to note from my survey that while most teachers felt that mixed ability most favoured this ability range, a few expressed concern about 'losing the pupils in the middle' who 'tend to get forgotten' in the mixed ability class. Perhaps this is because more teacher effort is directed towards the 'high' and 'low' levels of ability simply because these have been traditionally recognised as requiring some level of special attention in a mixed ability class.

Some reservations were expressed in relation to the 'more able' pupils again in common with historical evidence about mixed ability teaching. There was a complaint among some of those interviewed that 'the top kids are not stretched enough' and a certain wistfulness was expressed about the concept of a 'top stream' where 'language and literature work can be refined.' But on balance, teachers reinforced the advantages to 'more able' pupils of mixed ability:

'the more able children, if they're all put together, miss out on a lot of experience...they learn a lot from helping others, particularly in oral situations, drama and discussion. It's wrong to assume that the more able kids have got it all there.'

The value of mixed ability grouping was supported by a number of 'able' pupils (interviewed by Vanessa Culver, see footnote p.29) who had experienced both mixed ability and setted groups for English, exemplified by this comment:

'I think [mixed ability] is great. It means that you can work with people of different abilities and help them. It helps me because the first stage is learning how to do the things. The second stage is telling people how to do them yourself.' (Adrian, age 11, Year 7.)

Indeed this final point seems to be a crucial one in the educational case for mixing ability levels: that inherent in the nature of learning is the ability to demonstrate or practise your knowledge, understanding and skills in a subject. One of the most powerful ways for pupils to achieve this is by **teaching** others to know, to understand and to do something. This is not simply the prerogative of the more able (as Adrian implies above), but is within the capability of **all** pupils. In a mixed ability class, the repository of collective learning is likely to be considerably more diverse than that found in a more selective grouping: hence everyone has something to teach to members of their peer group; and everyone has something to learn from each other.

(ii) Recognising pupils as individual learners

One of the most common and sustained arguments among English teachers for mixed ability, both historically and in the sample I interviewed, was for recognising all children in a class of whatever grouping as individual learners with differing needs, aptitudes, abilities, interests and levels of motivation. Although this argument clearly figures for any grouping, the principle of heterogeneity **inherent** in grouping a mixed ability class makes much more explicit the differences between children. Richard Mills writing in 1977, deconstructed the term 'stream' to reveal how both explicitly and implicitly, teachers will tend to homogenise children deemed to be of similar ability:

A stream of water generally flows in the same direction over the same ground, at the same speed. A stream of children, it is implied, is expected to pursue activities corporately. The class generally works on the same material at the same speed. In other words, streaming is an organizational device and promotes a teaching style which minimises individual differences. Mixed ability grouping forces us to notice and take into account the specific strengths and weaknesses, interests and idiosyncrasies of individual children, and treat each according to need. (Mills 1977.)

This idea that mixed ability forces teachers to notice differences between pupils, is something which is of particular relevance to the teaching of English. The essential difficulty of defining ability in English because of the range and diversity of qualities and competences it requires, implies that the same child might be excellent at oral work, moderately able in imaginative writing, but rather weak in the 'clerical' skills of handwriting, spelling and punctuation. As one teacher expressed it, 'English as a subject requires such different aptitudes and skills…what can we use as the basis for banding or setting?' This view that mixed ability means pupils are not so likely to be prejudged or stereotyped according to an assumed homogenised level of ability across all four language modes, was endorsed by a number of the teachers I interviewed, of which these comments were typical:

> 'One of my Year 7 girls at the moment isn't particularly able in her writing; get her up there in a debate and she's very well informed. She can hold her own among the brightest children because she's got opinions, she has got ideas; she has found out by listening to documentaries and she can hold her own.'

> 'Often I think the most successful pupils [in English] can often be your 'less able' when they write about a personal experience. The best piece of writing of one of my weaker pupils was about the death of her grandmother and how that affected her. She somehow managed to find the correct spelling, the correct grammar…because she was pouring forth on something she had never spoken about to anybody and it was really very powerful.'

Thus the use of mixed ability not only forces English teachers to notice the differences *between* pupils, but also to notice the different abilities *within* each pupil. It enables teachers to recognise the complex, diverse, and indefinable nature of ability in English, from which no pupil is completely excluded.

(iii) Relevance to English

Perhaps what most distinguishes the current case for mixed ability from its 1970s rationale, is its relevance to the nature of English teaching. Throughout the 1980s, English as a secondary school subject was the focus of intense critical scrutiny and debate at a political, academic and pedagogical level. English is **not** a subject which is easy to define or categorise in terms of content, understanding and skill areas despite recent attempts to do so by working parties in English for the National Curriculum (DES 1989). Hence the case for mixed ability has now to be made in the light of competing views about what English *is*.

However unstable the identity of English as a subject might be, there **was** some consensus among the teachers I interviewed about what they are trying to do. If pupils are to make sense of the post-modernist notion that a subject may be studied from different perspectives, and that there is no 'correct' or definitive body of knowledge that can be called English, then they must learn to become self-sufficient, flexible and reflexive learners, able to take some responsibility for their learning and to have some independence of critical judgement. For this reason, English teachers emphasise the importance of equipping pupils with the communication skills and competences, the awareness and sensitivities to allow them to make their own routes through the world. Such aims do not require that pupils learn roughly at the same rate and level. Indeed, the variety and flexibility necessary both in subject matter and in teaching approaches means that English can offer a wide spectrum of learning opportunities from which pupils can benefit at their own pace and level.

In my interviews with English teachers, many examples were given of the compatibility between the pluralist and eclectic nature of English, and the flexible nature of mixed ability grouping, but two in particular stood out. The first was the role of speaking and listening which has become centralised within English teaching since the inception of GCSE in 1986, and which thrives upon the range and polyphony of a mixed ability class:

> 'The moment that oracy became a central issue within English it seemed to me there was no way you could any longer stream groups sensibly, because the mixed ability classroom provides you with a very rich range of audiences, whereas the streamed classroom (however you go about it) ends up with a social class catchment which makes up your stream...that's a narrowing of audience in terms of language repertoires, background interests, life experiences and so forth.'

The second example is the enhanced role of pair or group work in the mixed ability setting. This is not only valuable as a pedagogical tool to enable mixed ability groups to function properly, but also is perceived by both teachers and pupils as a means of developing a mutually interdependent sense of social and linguistic competence:

> 'Mixed groups are good because children of different abilities challenge each other more...they can't take things so much for granted...they are forced to clarify their points, justify their assumptions....get through to each other.'

The reasons cited today by English teachers and their pupils in their support of mixed ability groupings are not startlingly new or revelatory. But a clear theme in their comments is the importance of polyphony and self-sufficiency in learning – the power to be able to listen to a range of different voices, and to communicate effectively – with people who are **like** themselves, and with people who are very **unlike** themselves.

How to teach mixed ability

In some of the mixed ability halls we visited, the children were being taught as if they were a homogeneous group, much of their experience being direct class teaching aimed at the middle of the range. In others, the work was so finely individualised that the class rarely came together for a collective experience. (The Bullock Report 1975.)

This comment from the Bullock Report (Bullock 1975) highlights a traditional difficulty with mixed ability grouping – that it is not at all obvious how such a group should be taught. It may not be surprising that teachers struggled through the 1970s to find a pedagogical approach which simultaneously fostered a sense of group identity and allowed for individual differentiation. Did teachers of mixed ability pupils eventually resolve the difficulties observed by Bullock and discover an appropriate and distinctive set of strategies?

My own experience of teaching mixed ability groups during my main block teaching practice at The Banbury School in 1978 certainly highlights some of these difficulties. In one of the two 'mixed ability' halls at the school, I remember observing a number of powerfully led lessons by a range of charismatic and experienced teachers who generally taught the whole class 'from the front'. Impressed by their example, and awe-inspired by their prior knowledge of the classes I was to teach, I strove to emulate their teacher-led approaches. In the case of one 'third year' mixed ability class in particular, this proved a disastrous mistake. Resentful of my presence and of the loss of their regular teacher, the class refused to allow me the right to teach them as a whole class. One confrontation followed another until by the mid-way, half-term point, I feared that I could no longer face them. Resolution and relief came in the form of advice from my tutor: 'Stop trying to teach them as a whole class. They are a collection of individuals. Look for an approach where they are working not for you, but for **themselves**.'

The passage of time has perhaps over-glorified that moment and the weeks proceeding it. But my decision to introduce individualised project-based work with a common theme, and drawing upon a class 'library' for research and reference acted as a breakthrough both for my relationship with that group of pupils, and for my development as a teacher. The release from trying to be a sergeant major, a ringleader, a sage and an entertainer all in one role, was deeply liberating. As well as discovering my personal predilection for a facilitative style of teaching, I realised the value of the individualised learning paradigm as one strategy at least, for effective teaching of English to mixed ability groups.

This example from personal experience also illustrates two features of the period: the first that the introduction of mixed ability groupings in comprehensive schools did stimulate an intellectual and pedagogical debate in Higher Education about the need for new teaching paradigms; the second that this debate did not immediately bring with it an obvious corresponding change in teaching styles and practices. Has experience of mixed ability during the last twenty years brought with it any further insights about how it should be taught? Is there a need for a 'rethink' of approaches to mixed ability if it is to survive the current trend in favour of selective grouping? My own training for teaching English to mixed ability groups was predicated on the notion that a fundamental shift away from a paradigm of whole class teaching was essential. Indeed, a review of the fairly extensive literature written during the 1970s reveals a broad advocation of a model of individualised learning for mixed ability teaching. There is space here to give only a brief synopsis of some of the common features of this model, developed by *inter alia* Kelly (1974, 1978), Adams and Pearce (1974), Mills (1977).

Despite the extensive literature advocating and describing this approach to mixed ability teaching, evidence from that period suggests that teachers were reluctant to forsake the more traditional model of mainly whole class teaching. This was noted back in 1978 in an HMI working party's report (HMI 1978) on teaching mixed ability groups, which observed that lessons for such classes frequently took the form of a whole class being taught as a single unit with the lesson content aimed at the middle ranges of ability (or even just below) and the same task set for all pupils. The consequence of this was obvious: pupils of 'low' ability as well as pupils of 'high' ability were unlikely to be receiving the most appropriate range of materials and teaching. The report pinpointed how demanding mixed ability grouping is upon teachers, requiring considerable 'scholarship and intellectual resources' for the most able and appropriate remedial strategies together with 'sympathetic insight and patience' for the least able:

> Mixed ability teaching requires special qualities in the teachers involved. Catering adequately for the full ability range within each mixed ability group calls for more sophisticated professional skills than does teaching in more traditional forms of organisation. (HMI 1978.)

The report concluded that when class teaching predominates with a mixed ability group providing no differentiation in the kinds of learning opportunity available, 'it must follow that individual requirements are not being met.' It was this issue of differentiation which had triggered the higher education debate on teaching methodology and hence on the kinds of preparation teachers might need to teach mixed ability effectively.

Little research material exists since the 1970s to show whether or not there has been a significant shift in the methodologies of teachers of mixed ability English classes to take account of this need for 'differentiation'. Therefore it seemed timely in my own research to find out how English teachers practise mixed ability teaching, and to what extent the model of individualised learning is still considered to be appropriate in today's context. In my in-depth interviews with over twenty experienced English teachers of mixed ability classes from a range of comprehensive schools, I discovered a loose consensus on the principles essential to effective mixed ability teaching, summarised in the following boxed sections. The implications of these principles are considered in the two sections (**A** and **B**) which follow:

Principles of effective mixed ability English teaching in the 1990s

(A) *Attention to the needs of each individual pupil*
- awareness that the class is a 'collection of individuals' with individual needs, interests, aptitudes, abilities
- realistic teacher expectations of each pupil
- differentiated outcomes for assignments set, and where possible, differentiated resource material, methods, class and group activities
- close monitoring and evaluation of each individual pupil

(B) *A broad spectrum of teaching approaches*
- the 'essential' role of whole class teaching
- the vital role of grouping pupils drawing upon a range of grouping strategies
- a good range of resources: written, printed, audio-visual
- the wide-ranging, 'flexible' role of the teacher

(A) *Attention to the needs of each individual pupil*

The importance of recognising the individual needs of each pupil in a mixed ability class has been heightened in recent years by the requirements of the English Orders of the National Curriculum. This makes explicit the need for teachers to ensure that differentiation between pupils, and assessment of the differing abilities of an individual pupil, is achieved in their teaching.

Among the teachers I interviewed there was a 'received wisdom' that English is traditionally a subject which tends less to differentiate by *task* than by *outcome*. Thus, a class will share the same stimulus, and work on the same task, but the standards attained by pupils in the resulting pieces of work will relate to their abilities. Most of the teachers interviewed believed that differentiation by outcome was both a valuable and justifiable practice in mixed ability teaching if carefully managed:

'In English you judge children by their outcomes. You can teach the subject in the same way to all children and what they achieve can be individually monitored and negotiated. There is no limit on what the most able children can achieve by outcome in a mixed ability class.'

'A lot of differentiation can happen by outcome if the task is carefully devised. Most pupils can have access to it and can achieve, but you do have to have extension work, fall-back plans and more user-friendly materials to cope. It does create problems for teachers.'

Among just a few of those teachers interviewed there was the view that **differentiation by outcome,** whilst relatively straightforward as far as organisation, planning and assessment were concerned, was inadequate if it was the only differentiating mechanism:

'It has the distinct drawback of disadvantaging the less able pupils. Also, the task may not offer the more able pupils an adequate challenge.'

These teachers felt that **differentiation by task** could be more finely attuned to individual students, but the drawbacks were that it relied heavily on the teacher's correct assessment of the pupils' needs and abilities, which in turn depended on meticulous organising and monitoring of pupils' work. It seems from the findings of my research at least, that in general English teachers today are sceptical of the individualised programmes of learning heralded by the mixed ability pundits of the 1970s – partly from experience of their complex practical demands, and partly because they preclude areas of learning in English which the collective class experience can develop:

'I think individualised learning is wrong for much of what we do – for example, there's a lot of drama in English. There are wonderful things which can happen with whole classes.'

Perhaps a revised understanding of 'individualised learning' is emerging:

'It seems to me that the ideal approach would be to offer a range of levels of tasks rather than wholly individualised tasks. Guidance could be offered as to the most suitable work for any one pupil, by negotiation. In addition, the strategies necessary for the completion of the task could be made available to all pupils or just to those who needed assistance.'

Undoubtedly 'attention to the individual needs of a pupil' has always been a maxim of the English teacher responsible for mixed ability classes. However, there may have been a shift away from the practice of individualised methods of learning in the 1970s, towards the greater use of a collective classroom approach today, with attention to individual needs focussed on monitoring and assessment of the progress of each pupil, both in terms of approaches to tasks and to outcomes.

(B) *A broad spectrum of teaching approaches*

Two features stand out as characteristic of the 1990s approach to teaching English to mixed ability groups. The first is teachers' recognition of the value of a pluralistic, eclectic methodology which rejects any single learning paradigm as 'the answer'. Clearly experience has shown teachers that they can be very effective in using a wide variety of teaching strategies with mixed ability classes:

'I don't see why you have to marry one teaching methodology with one grouping system. There is no reason why a mixed ability class shouldn't listen to a teacher from the front, some of the time. There are a number of very experienced teachers around now who have tried it all ways.'

'A teacher needs to adopt many roles – providing the means, proposing a model, defining a course of action – those are all roles which are part of the armoury of mixed ability teaching.'

The view that a teacher begins first and foremost with an understanding and knowledge of her class as a collection of individuals, and ascertains the methodology and scheme of work she will use accordingly, was a predominant theme in teachers' comments. English teachers like to feel that they have a repertoire of teaching strategies at their disposal which range along a continuum from, at one extreme, teacher-led, direct class teaching, through various forms of interactive, co-operative and group activity, to wholly individualised, negotiated, pupil-led learning at the other extreme.

The second feature which stands out as characteristic of 'the 1990s approach' is the conscious and expert consideration English teachers give to the range of ways of **grouping** pupils in a mixed ability class. While there is some concern about the necessity of manipulating grouping on **social** grounds ('a class is not truly 'mixed ability' if you are merely allowing kids to work in groups according to their ability – it just reinforces social stereotypes'), most of the discussion about grouping today focusses on its **educational** value. The importance of giving thought to

how pupils should be grouped was considered vital for achieving a stim-
ulating, varied and dynamic learning environment:

> 'Largely, [pupils] work in groups and it is important to check that the
> groups aren't always random or self-selected, but you can have an
> impact on what's done and how it's done by grouping according to gen-
> der, or to ability within the class, sometimes allowing friends to work
> together, sometimes making people who don't like each other work
> together.'

If English teachers are tending towards using common resource materials,
and on some occasions are also expecting pupils to undertake common
activities and assignments, then the deployment of varied grouping strategies may be essential in offering differing levels of stimulus, incentive
and mutual support: the mixed ability classroom offers this greater flexibility in the grouping process:

> 'There are times when I have engineered the class so that they are a
> mixed group, so that the weaker ones are supported by the more able
> ones....but there are also times when you have them reading 6-pack
> novels or whatever, where they will differentiate among themselves and
> they will find their own level.'

It appears that, since the 1970s, teachers have gained more confidence
and experience in recognising the many ways in which the manipulation
of group work can enrich learning in English. They can draw on their
experience to decide how particular grouping strategies best develop the
intricate 'mix' of abilities in each pupil.

Conclusions

The use of mixed ability in English, particularly in the lower school, has
been an almost unquestioned practice in many comprehensive schools
during the last two decades. With pressure from right wing groups of
politicians and educationalists to move schools towards selection by ability, and with the introduction of the Standard Assessment Tests (SATs),
mixed ability grouping has become increasingly hard to sustain. Part of
the problem for teachers of mixed ability English – both for the committed few and for the less committed majority – is that they have forgotten
how to articulate the case for it. Mixed ability has ceased to be an interesting issue, because it has been assimilated into routine practice.

I believe it is time for English teachers to resurrect the dialogue about
ways of grouping pupils by ability – to start with asking about the nature

of and meaning of 'ability'; and about how pupils most effectively learn to acquire the diverse competences, understandings, critical awareness and sensitivities which are part of the amorphous subject of English. Within a post-modernist vision of education, no single system can ever be heralded as 'the answer' especially if it offers itself as a universalising truth. However, a pedagogical framework which foregrounds the value of promoting the differences, and the connections between individual pupils; which acknowledges learning to be reflexive, recursive and fluid; which encourages self-empowerment and independence in a changing and often chaotic socio-economic climate, is at least worthy of defence. Let's begin to discuss mixed ability again.

THE 1970s MODEL OF INDIVIDUALISED LEARNING

The nature of English:	– various redefinitions of the subject, e.g: a cross-curricular 'strand' in an integrated Humanities programme; – an integrated subject: no artificial 'divides' between language–literature, or between oracy, reading and writing.
Role of learner:	– autonomous, independent, self-directed; – capable of negotiating their own learning; – able to work individually or in small groups.
Role of teachers:	– a helper, adviser, facilitator, extra 'resource'; also monitors, records and assesses individual effort and achievement; – no longer a lecturer or 'knowledge expert'; – end to 'chalk and talk'.
Nature of work:	– often project work or workshop-based; – on themes, topics or literary texts: *either* common framework for class, e.g. common learning aims and objectives; common programme of work *but* incorporating a range of choice of activities and assignments; *or* use of individualised programmes of work based on work sheets, work cards and so on; – differentiated resource materials and tasks.
Methods of working:	– usually self-directed using a variety of forms of inquiry, research and investigation, e.g. library research; interviews; group discussion and problem-solving; role-play.
Work scheduling:	– half-termly 'units' or 'blocks' of 3 or 4 weeks for project work; – double periods favoured; – an end to the 'Grammar on Tuesday' approach.
Resources and equipment:	– classroom to be very well equipped to facilitate 'active', independent learning: e.g. a class library, a 'quiet room' for discussion and tape-recording, a set of portable tape recorders, access to computer work stations.
Classroom arrangements:	– based on progressive primary school practice: flexible, mobile, and adaptable; – teacher's desk in corner – no longer 'at the front'.

CHAPTER 4

English and ability: writing

'A noble effort of the imagination',
'Better work, but watch your spelling',
'The best first novel of this year',
'GCSE achievement at Level 7',
'I chose this as my best piece because it was exciting and had a good ending',
'All the letters sent from my office I have to correct myself, and that is because English is taught so bloody badly'.

What do such comments actually mean? In their different ways, all of these attempt to engage with the qualities revealed in written texts and to report a judgement – for the author, for the record, for the reading public or for posterity. From the sum of such judgements we derive the concept of ability in writing, grounded in a view of what a child of a certain age, a 'literate' person, a skilled adult or a professional novelist, say, can or should be able to do. The process is so established and automatic that it is easy to talk as though 'ability' is an absolute quality inherent in a text.

In fact, though, the kind of ability seen in 'Thirty years ago, Marseilles lay burning in the sun one day' or 'Onc upon a time a prinss livd in a cassl' is attributed to the text by the reader. To evaluate any piece of writing involves bringing to it a set of related reading experiences (the opening of other major novels or young children's awareness of fairy tales, in these examples) which have combined to create a model for the reader of what such text 'should' or 'might' be like. Without such expectations, reasoned evaluation becomes difficult or impossible. For example, when I presented adult readers with the openings of similar stories written by children, by authors of books for young people and by adult novelists, they were unwilling to judge or even to comment on them because they could not be sure which were which. They were afraid of making a

'mistake' in judging the relative 'quality' of one text (written in a particular context) by standards appropriate to another. Responding takes into
account both our models of texts and the anticipated responses of other
readers within an 'interpretive community', those whose readings are
conditioned by their shared 'strategies for writing texts' (Fish 1980,
p.171): Dickens scholars or specialists in the language of five-year-olds in
the two examples above.

This process can be experienced practically by reading these two
extracts and considering what marks of ability are found there.

> We have recently finished some work in History. It was about diseases in the
> 17th to 18th century and what medicines were introduced to cure these dis-
> eases. Penicillin was the main thing they wrote about. How it was invented
> who invented it, how it was tested etc, and what illnesses it was used on. We
> also wrote about famous men and women who during the Crimea helped the
> wounded soldiers. I found it interesting because it shows how medicine has
> advanced since then for the better.

> Last week after waching an exstreamly interesting programe on the television
> investagateing Indian familys I decided to learn even more about arranged
> marrages so I discussed what I have learnt to a friend at school who herself is
> Indian and will have her husband chosen for her by her parents, I arsked her:
> 'Dose it not worrie you that the man to whome you will marrie might be crule
> to you and how can you love a man that you have never seen nor know about?'
> Kuldip, (my friend), replied: 'It dose not suprise me that you find my religion
> hard to understand because you, being English have to choose your own part-
> ner for marrige and I also find your English traditions or ways very difficult to
> understand.'

What do we make of these passages? As we read them 'blind', our
notions of the quality of the writing will be inseparable from our construction of the 'implied' writers (what we imagine their age, ability,
gender, and attitude to the task to be), our expectations of such writing,
and the comparisons we make between the two pieces and others within our experience. Such constructions may be confirmed or questioned
when we hear the views of others. For example, when we know that
both pieces were offered as samples of roughly 'average' work by 15-
year-olds (APU 1983), how does this affect our reading of them? As
both were chosen as examples of texts in which writers report about
something recently learned, can we predict how they would respond to
different written tasks? Both were graded four on a seven-point scale
(together with a quarter of the population tested) but clearly the actual
'qualities' that led each to be so placed are very different. Is it significant that the second of these, rather than the first, was selected by John
Marenbon to illustrate his claim 'that there is such concern today at low
standards of English'? Marenbon makes what he considers an objective

judgement that 'The writer of this passage is obviously intelligent and inquisitive, but his weak grasp of grammar, punctuation and spelling prevents him from writing with clarity or ease' (Marenbon 1987, p.6). How far do we share this opinion, and what does it tell us in turn about Marenbon? He has brought to his reading of the passage (as we do) expectations about 'average' ability, a particular rank-order of criteria, beliefs about writing ('prevents him...') and a dominant assumption about the relationship between teaching and learning ('English is badly taught, and...used to be taught better' (Marenbon 1987, p.8)). Any judgements of written texts that we or others make are themselves 'texts' that are equally open to be 'read'.

Why identifying ability in writing is problematic

Most of those like Marenbon, concerned about 'standards' of writing in general and of schoolchildren in particular, assume that assessing the quality of writing is easier and more reliable than it is. The difficulties of locating and assessing writing ability can be swiftly outlined. Estimates depend on what precisely is being judged, by whom, how and in what context, by what criteria and for what purpose.

1. The term 'writing ability' is not the simple unitary concept that some examiners and politicians would like to pretend. Rather, it is a convenient blanket phrase for a complex of separate interlocking abilities, compositional (such as generating ideas, organising them, drawing on personal and secondhand experiences, making rhetorical choices) and secretarial (transcribing, editing, revising, correcting). As will be suggested in the following points, it is easy to emphasise some parts of the writing process at the expense of others when evaluating a piece of work, as in one researcher's comment on secondary pupils who 'understood the essence of the task but who could not clothe their ideas in adequate literary language' (Neville 1988, p.125).

2. Comments on ability are inevitably subjective. For over a century, evidence has accumulated that different markers rate the same text differently and that the same marker rates a text differently on different occasions. We frame the texts we read according to our own personalities, and our judgements frequently say more about the reader's assumptions than about the writer and the writing (as in the case of Marenbon above). 'What we see in children's writing depends on the questions we ask of it, the categories we apply to it, or the framework that makes sense of it' (Protherough 1983, p.28).

3. The criteria used for assessing ability are shifting and culturally determined. The first Assessment of Performance Unit's primary language report demonstrated convincingly that the apparent relative difficulty of four writing tasks changed dramatically according to the criteria by which the work was assessed (APU 1981, pp.108–9). The extent of cultural influences on criteria was vividly demonstrated by the failure of the international Written Composition Study to achieve the expected comparability of performance between students of different languages and educational systems. 'The international framework setting standards of good writing is interpreted differently in different systems of education…performance in writing is part of a culture' (Purves 1992, p.200). Like those shifting and shifty words 'literate' and 'illiterate' (Levine 1986), concepts of quality in writing vary according to the community and the technology through which writing is carried out and communicated. When children come from families that share and reinforce the literary ethos dominant in a culture, they are likely to be seen as 'good' writers. Heath has shown clearly how different cultural groups in the same country vary in their perceptions of 'appropriate' writing (Heath 1983), and investigations have demonstrated how apparently 'objective' tests of writing ability can discriminate against candidates from ethnic minorities (White 1985, pp.72–83).

4. Estimates of ability are heavily influenced by the purpose for which the operation is being carried out: diagnosing the needs of an individual, monitoring the success of a teaching programme, measuring one group against another, or illustrating an ideological point. Frequently, however, there are underlying, and perhaps unintended, implications. For example, the Newsom Report said that an English course ('vocational in the best possible way') 'should provide a good foundation for workmanlike English in that it will enable boys and girls in later life to read instructions or pass on messages, or write a letter, or jot down a record' (Ministry of Education 1963, p.159). Any assessment of written ability in those terms would be inevitably restricted. Equally, during the vogue for what was called 'creative' writing, estimates of ability tended to devalue other written modes (Protherough 1978). At the time of writing, the furore over testing the National Curriculum largely turns on teachers' perceptions that the tests being imposed have a political rather than an educational purpose.

5. There is no consensus over what 'good' writing looks like in any absolute sense. Studies have demonstrated how different academic disciplines and professions value different written conventions and procedures and offer distinct 'models' of what 'good writing' is thought to be (Becher 1987, 1989). The field of literature might be expected to offer agreed

models, but there are many notorious cases of texts that have been interpreted and valued by critics in contradictory ways. Those believing that it is possible neatly to define as models 'texts of central importance to the literary heritage' (National Curriculum Council 1993) should be warned by the ever-shifting curriculum of examination forms in schools and of universities (Protherough 1989, pp.82–93). Even where there is broad agreement about which texts should be studied, this frequently conceals major variations in opinion about their merits and the markers of such merit. At the pedagogic level, changes in the way that writing is taught go hand in hand with changes in the kind of pupils' work that is selected for praise. Few English teachers today share the enthusiasm shown by Ballard in 1921 when praising what he thought an 'outstanding' essay (Protherough 1983, pp.21–3).

6. Writing is heavily, indeed dominantly, influenced by the situation in which it is carried out, the purpose for which it is written and the topic. The first version of the national curriculum for English summed this up in the words 'Language competence is dependent on the task: children will show different ability on tasks of different kinds.' (DES 1989, 17.25.) Students who write well on one subject can be rated poorly on another. For example, there was little relationship between the 'content' scores on different topics in the Scottish National Assessment of English (Neville 1988, pp.117–8, 209). With older students, there was a very low correlation between the scores achieved on two pieces of writing (one personal and one analytic) by potential university entrants (White 1985, pp.117–8). Some students are skilful when writing on topics or in modes that rarely appear in educational settings. Harpin's study of a range of variables in the writing of junior school pupils found that the most important factor was the context or situation of the writing (Harpin 1976).

The existence of such difficulties as these does not mean, of course, that the tasks of defining ability in writing or of assessing it should not be attempted, only that we should be careful about claiming too much for them. What follows considers the specifically educational implications of thinking about quality in writing.

The educational context

Public concern over the quality of children's writing and the shortcomings of English teaching, regularly aired in the media, has both sensible and discreditable sides. Because writing ability is so clearly linked to thinking, learning and living in contemporary society, it is right to see it as central to the educational process. On the other hand, the recurrent scare stories of falling standards, used for their own purposes by politicians and the popular press (with headlines like 'You can't write proper', 'Save the Queen's English' and 'English teaching is awful, claims Charles'), are both unsoundly based and unhelpful in improving teaching and learning. Identical criticisms have been common for even longer than English has existed as a separate school subject. Early this century it was 'abundantly proved that the average public schoolboy cannot write good English' and that such students left school at 18 or 19 'able hardly to write a coherent sentence, with no knowledge of punctuation, no vocabulary, no power of expression...' (Peers 1914, p.15, Mais 1914, pp.187–8). Over seventy years ago the Newbolt Report quoted the laments of different employers that 'young employees are so hopelessly deficient in their command of English' (Board of Education 1921, para. 77). 'All complained, often bitterly, of defects in spelling, punctuation, vocabulary, and sentence structure' (Board of Education 1921, para. 137). Those who pride themselves on their own ability with the written language have always tended to see surface errors as some kind of moral weakness, for which bad teaching is to be blamed.

It is ironic, but perhaps not surprising, that the same prescriptive views are the ones that students have internalised. When young children describe what they have to do in order to write well, their comments emphasise neatness and avoidance of mistakes (Czerniewska 1992, pp.78–80, Thornton 1986, p.22). Asked what they saw as the most important qualities in writing, 15-year-olds predominantly mentioned 'the correct management of surface features such as spelling, neatness and punctuation', whereas assessors found appropriateness, style and interest considerably more significant. Contrary to popular opinion, the APU survey concluded that 'schools are not failing to instruct pupils in the need for control over so called "basic skills", nor are pupils failing to heed such lessons' (White 1986, pp.14–18).

To understand such differences in perception about writing in school, we need to be clear that our responses will vary according to two main factors: (i) our model of the writing process and (ii) our view of the educational purposes of instruction in writing.

(i) Notions of where merit is to be sought will depend on the views we have of those two linked processes of writing and of reading, the balance we keep between 'product' and 'process'. Those who believe in short national tests of writing ability are following in the footsteps of what was once called the 'new criticism', with its belief that meaning resided in the text itself and that the author's (and reader's) intentions and situation are irrelevant. They would see a student's writing as a finished product to be analysed and judged objectively. They might ignore such issues as the author's background, the circumstances of the writing, what the author meant to say or might have said, or whether other readers might judge the work differently.

By contrast, those English teachers who have been influenced by reader-response theories are more likely to believe that they 'construct' the work in the act of reading it. They will see a piece of writing as part of a process, in which the reader's view of the author's situation and purposes and the reader's response to the text will all be part of its 'meaning'. They believe that they are reacting personally to the work; that the idea of an impartial, objective reading is a fallacy. One has to learn what is meant by reading student writing, just as one has to learn what is meant by reading a literary text of a particular kind. They would attempt to bring together writing and reading as twin, related acts of meaning-making: 'Reading is itself a kind of writing, or writing is a trope for the act of reading' (Miller 1983, p.41); 'Readers and writers are partners, just as reading and writing are connected, interactive processes' (Maimon 1983, p.111).

(ii) A second major source of variation concerns the relative importance attached to those two purposes of work in English, and of writing in particular: socialising into a particular culture and discipline, and developing the individuality, the personal 'voice', of each student. A concern for the former dwells on the need to acquire skills required in the adult world, to learn the conventions of spelling, syntax and punctuation, and to shape style in accordance with models that are seen as worthy of imitation. Ability in this sense may be assessed (particularly in the United States, as in the Test of Standard Written English) by multiple-choice tests in error-location and correction, though it is doubtful whether those who are successful in these are necessarily good writers. An emphasis on the latter aims at educating students to think for themselves, to respond personally to what they read and to be imaginative and original in their writing. A desire to give greater emphasis to the first at the expense of the second was manifest in the remit given to the National Curriculum Council for revising the English component of the National Curriculum, and in the Council's response. One of the four identified 'needs' was to 'define more clearly the basic writing skills and grammatical knowledge which pupils needed to master and the variety of ways in which competence in spelling could be developed' (NCC 1993, p.iii). Throughout the document runs a 'requirement' for pupils to use Standard English correctly, 'in order to enhance the communicator skills necessary for social and professional development' (NCC 1993, p.9).

Within this context, the following sections examine some of the ways in which comparative ability and the growth of ability in writing have been estimated in the past and look forward to consider the implications for the National Curriculum and its testing.

On what basis is ability in writing to be assessed?

'Writing ability is the school subject which is most difficult to assess' (Wesdorp et al 1982, p.299). In view of the difficulties outlined above, it is no surprise that encyclopaedias on testing have such heavy coverage of a multitude of tests for reading and almost nothing on tests of writing. It is possible to detach and to test individual 'skills', like spelling or the ability to identify syntactical errors, but this is not the same thing as assessing the ability to write. Pupils' apparent ability in tests of spelling, punctuation or syntax is frequently quite different from their performance when their own connected writing is examined (Neville 1988, pp.112–13, 116–17).

How do we define the tasks by which schoolchildren's ability in writing is to be determined? What a student can do can really only be judged by looking at the whole body of work produced and revised over a period of time, and even that judgement will omit the kinds of writing not publicly attempted or deliberately rejected. The Assessment of Performance Unit selected modes for testing on the principle that they should be 'representative' of what children were 'expected to write' in school. These tasks were defined by different dimensions: narrative and descriptive distinguished from reflective and analytical, personal from secondhand subject matter, and literary from functional purposes.

Tests of first-draft writing, however carefully set up, deny too many of the principles that underlie our understanding and teaching of writing. For many years, ability in writing at age 16 was judged by single pieces of work (traditionally lumped together under vague terms like 'composition' or 'essay') in one of four modes (narrative, descriptive, discursive or argumentative), as though these categories were divinely ordained and all equal. What was assessed was the student's ability, within a time limit, to understand the hidden assumptions of the task, then to formulate, express and organise in appropriate form a set of ideas on some artificially prescribed topic, like 'getting and spending' or 'a woman's place is in the home'. Many of the examiner-pleasing skills had little to do with actual writing ability, and it was hardly surprising that examiners frequently reported on the lifelessness, the 'rather thin quality' of work submitted.

In reaction against this, it has become conventional to suggest that 'success' should be defined in terms of ability to control a wide range of different genres or modes, with appropriate registers and rhetorical conventions. In the 1970s, the Bullock Report said 'We believe that progress in writing throughout the school years should be marked by an increasing differentiation in the kinds of writing a pupil can successfully tackle' (DES 1975, 11.8). The GCSE regulations for 1984 all insist on the need for students to be given opportunities 'to write in a wide range of styles and forms', with a rough distinction being made between 'imaginative' personal writing about experiences ('what they feel and imagine') and 'factual' writing (involving ability to 'understand, order and present facts, ideas and opinions'). These will be tested in examination and in a coursework folder, which may include (according to NEAB suggestions) different kinds of stories, poems and plays for distinct audiences, letters, studies of media texts, autobiography, articles, interview projects and reviews or other responses to reading. Three issues are still under debate. First, is range a dominant criterion, outweighing marked ability in a few modes? Second, are there, in fact, a limited number of written genres that are somehow 'fixed', or do 'generic forms vary in significant ways depending upon their site'? (Gilbert 1992, pp.78–9.) Third, should students deliberately be 'taught' the particular structures of these, and should they be assessed on their ability to replicate them? (Reid 1987.)

Although there is no agreement about any 'hierarchy' of genres, in which the acquisition of some forms precedes that of others, it is conventionally believed that some written tasks are 'easier' than others, especially for schoolchildren. As Richard Andrews puts it, 'There is still a general feeling that – up to age sixteen or so – students write better stories than arguments' (Andrews 1989, p.1, Freedman and Pringle 1984) and there is clear evidence that they enjoy argumentative writing much less than more 'imaginative' topics (APU 1982, pp.103–4). The attainment targets of the National Curriculum assume that narrative writing will precede argument and exposition. However, such global judgements can obscure two facts. First, any mode or genre ranges from simple to complex functions and involves abilities at different levels. The demands of narrative in handling dialogue or movements in time, for example, can be greater than those of straightforward factual reporting. A general term like 'argument', as Stratta and Dixon have pointed out, disguises a range of necessary distinctions of different complexity (Dixon and Stratta 1982). Second, students differ in their perceptions of the relative difficulty of certain subjects: 'there are few tasks which are uniformly 'hard' or 'easy' for either age group', 11 or 15 (White 1986, p.9).

Attempts to refine the assessment of writing ability

Studies show that assessment of writing can be influenced by such irrelevant factors as children's first names, their gender and appearance, and their handwriting (Wood and Napthali 1975, Briggs 1980). It is not surprising, then, that unease about the unreliability and subjectivism of 'general impression' (or 'holistic') marking of students' writing has resulted in various attempts to make assessment more precise. The advantages and weaknesses of some of these can be briefly summarised.

(i) *Creation of rating scales* Organising such scales was one of the first systematic attempts to assist teachers in assessment by providing graded examples. Pieces of children's writing (usually on the same or a similar topic) that are considered 'typical' of different levels of performance are ranked in order, normally based on the pooled judgements of a number of teachers or examiners. William Boyd was responsible for the first major attempt at such a scale in 1924, and he was so sure of the ratings arrived at by his panel that he claimed 'objective sureness' for them, 'the definite expression of a communal expert opinion which is the very essence of a standard of judgement' (Boyd 1924, pp.36–70). However, later experiments in giving some of Boyd's samples to teachers, examiners and students have found extreme variations in the rank order they give compared with those of 1924 (Protherough 1983, pp.190–5). Indeed, examining the scales of different periods offers a graphic indication of how our notions of ability in writing can change. The shift of criteria underlying the changes in ranking is made explicit by comparing Boyd's markers ('adult', 'elevated style', 'detached point of view', 'rhetorical devices') with those of a 1965 scale (LATE 1965) with its emphasis on 'sincerity', 'spontaneity', 'vividness', 'imaginative coherence', and 'personally creative' language. Perhaps the most recent large-scale attempt to exemplify levels of ability by publishing actual examples was made by the Assessment of Performance Unit (APU 1983). A similar principle has underpinned the attempts of GCSE boards to moderate internal assessment of student written work. By presenting exemplar material illustrating the criteria which distinguish work at one grade level from that at others, the boards have tried to define what the characteristics (markers) are of written work at different levels. Such guides move from separate criteria towards generalisations introduced by such words as 'To be graded at this level a paper will...' or 'An essay will fall into this category if...'

(ii) *Multiple impression marking* One attempt to overcome the inconsistencies of individual judgements was to increase reliability by pooling the estimates of several markers concentrating on achievement rather than on

57

errors. An experiment at GCE level suggested that the pooled marks of three examiners were both more reliable and agreed better with teachers' estimates of their students than conventional marking (Britton et al 1966). When the Assessment of Performance Unit was set up in Britain, it was decided to use a combination of impression and analytic marking to assess the work of a wide range of pupils. The APU studies had scripts double marked, and assessors were instructed to read rapidly to make an overall judgement and not to reread or revise marks. Like so much research on assessment, however, multiple marking is almost wholly concerned with improving reliability and consistency and rarely questions the purposes of the assessment or what is actually being measured. Studies of reliability can show to what extent markers rate similarly and consistently, but not necessarily that their judgements are – in any objective sense – 'right'.

(iii) *Analytic rating* Proposals for analytic rating of compositions have sought to define more precisely the reader's focus of attention ('primary trait' scoring in the US). By attempting to rank separately the level of performance manifested in different sub-skills, such proposals claimed to be more precise and more helpful diagnostically (Diederich 1966). For example, working for the National Council for the Teaching of English in the 1970s, Cooper and Odell proposed that a piece of narrative writing could be judged in eleven separate ways (and 'marked', if necessary, on a five-point scale for each). They distinguished between six 'general' qualities (author's role, style or voice, central figure, background, sequence and theme), and five concerned with 'diction, syntax and mechanics' (wording, syntax, usage, punctuation, spelling) (Cooper and Odell 1977). In a simplified version, the APU established five analytic criteria: content, organisation, style and appropriateness, grammatical conventions and orthographic conventions.

Attempts to specify and clarify what marks 'quality' in writing are clearly welcome. However, any analytic schemes are also open to criticism. They presuppose that effective writing can be seen and evaluated as the sum of certain specified parts, but there is no evidence either that the measuring of certain skills necessarily gives an accurate guide to the overall quality of a text, or that quality in writing comes by the process of accumulating a variety of sub-skills. There is no real agreement about what the separate sub-skills are that contribute to effective writing, or about their relative importance, or about how far some of them (like 'originality') can be identified. In some cases there is doubt whether the categories as defined are discrete or overlapping (is it realistic, for example, to separate wording, syntax and usage?) At the classroom level, there is some danger, particularly in considering the 'mechanics', of negative 'error-counting' approaches rather than positively considering the merits of the work. This can lead to rating accurate but empty writing more highly than adventurous work that takes risks with vocabulary and syntax.

Development in ability

What we call development or growth in writing is distinct from natural processes like physical growth; it is a culturally-defined product, resulting both from deliberate instruction and from chance learning. As our grasp of what ability in writing means is so relative and shaky, it is hardly surprising that our understanding of how it increases is also uncertain. Ten years ago, citing examples of the way in which scholars write of development in reading, I said that these were 'essentially metaphorical', and went on:

> These overlapping terms like *developing, maturing, growing, deepening, refining, elaborating,* propose a focus for our attention, but do little more. The generalisations are rarely fleshed out with examples…What are our criteria for saying that one child's response is more 'developed' than it was a year ago, or that it is more 'mature' than another child's? (Protherough 1983, p.34.)

The same comments hold good of writing. There is a surprising lack of longitudinal studies that follow the work of children over a period of years, although there are a few case studies of individuals (Protherough 1986, pp.78–85; Harrison 1986). Theoretical models of writing and its development can make us more sensitive to particular features of language acquisition, but rarely attempt to map with any accuracy the actual development of individuals. There have been several attempts at an all-embracing design for discourse (e.g. Kinneavy 1971), some of them listed sketchily in what follows, providing templates that helpfully frame different aspects of development. However, they have not yet established that dream sequence, some sort of scale that might offer 'a reliable and nationally uniform measure of a pupil's progress' (Dearing 1993, para. 1.5).

James Moffett hypothesised that development was essentially concerned with increasing ability to handle abstraction, to cope with greater distance between the writer, the reader and the experience. He proposed a logical sequence for instruction in writing, together with a practical programme, that would move from the present and particular towards the abstract and hypothetical, but without examining empirically the degree of match between the teaching and the learners' developing ability (Moffett 1968). James Britton's view of expressive writing as an all-purpose bridge from speech to written forms that were then progressively specialised to cope with different functions along a continuum, with 'transactional' (informational and persuasive) writing at one extreme and 'poetic' (imaginative) at the other, was helpful to schools in calling attention to the unbalanced demands made of students (Britton et al 1975). However, the model proved less useful for categorising actual children's writing (much of which was found hard to classify or existed in mixed modes) or for charting just how ability in handling complex forms of writing was learned. Bereiter and Scardamalia have proposed that development is to be perceived in the ability to make successive features of the complex act of writing automatic and instinctive. Learning is marked by sufficient mastery of a particular process to enable the writer's attention to be diverted elsewhere. In their terms, the student's progress is revealed in greater awareness of the conventions appropriate to particular genres, of the likely reactions of an envisaged audience, of self-evaluation and of the possibilities of thinking through writing (Bereiter 1980). If texts in different genres have characteristic structures that permit different meanings to be made, as some theorists would argue, then development can be defined in terms of increased ability to select and use appropriate genres for written tasks (Christie 1987).

There have been a number of attempts to ground development in apparently objective linguistic markers, notably by Loban in his longitudinal study carried out in the United States (Loban 1963, 1976) and by Harpin with a team of teachers in the UK (Harpin 1976). The only agreed features associated with increasing maturity seem to be the hardly surprising ones of greater sentence length and the increasing use of more complex subordinate clauses. Hunt's view that lengthening T–units are associated with what he calls 'syntactical maturity' (Hunt 1970), which resulted in the brief popularity of teaching sentence-combining, misses the point unless the statistical record is accompanied by some qualitative analysis of what is said and how. Some excellent writing is done in short T–units; some of the worst and most convoluted bureaucratic prose in long ones (Williams 1979).

Models have been most helpful to teachers when grounded in 'signs of development' revealed in actual classroom writing. Dixon and Stratta, for example, have examined students' narrative writing in four dimensions: What counts as human experience? How is time handled in the narrative? How are people, places and situations contextualised for the reader? How are the different elements in the story integrated? (Dixon and Stratta 1986.) They follow this discussion into consideration of non-narrative modes, and particularly into argument, a topic taken further by Andrews in two research projects and in books like *Narrative and Argument*

(Andrews 1989, 1993). Perhaps the most ambitious model, and one close-ly related to the classroom process, has been the Crediton Project of Wilkinson and others. Evolving over some years, this model attempted to describe development in four related areas (cognitive, affective, moral and stylistic) and to offer examples drawn from the work of pupils aged seven, ten, eleven and thirteen (Wilkinson 1986).

The commonsense view is that ability increases with age, experience and instruction, but if this is true then the development is not regular. The Scottish National Assessment of English, for example, found that in gen-eral children made great advances in writing in the three years between Primary grades 4 and 7, but much less in the two years of transition between Primary 7 and Secondary 2. Although on average the secondary children wrote more, 'the language and style was not more mature and the content was not more rigorously presented' (Neville 1988, p.122). What about the students who, in the opinion of their teachers, fail to progress or even get worse rather than better?

Writing ability in the National Curriculum

Uncertainty about what ability in writing actually means, and how it can be measured, is reflected in two different versions of the National Curriculum, only separated from one another by four years. The Cox Committee framed Attainment Target 3 as 'A growing ability to construct and convey meaning in written language matching style to audience and purpose' (DES 1989). The proposed revision substituted 'The develop-ment of the ability to convey meaning effectively in written standard English' (NCC 1993). The second thus eliminated the notion of con-structing meaning (for oneself, perhaps) in favour of the straight commu-nication model, rejected by Cox ('written language...not limited to the communication of information' (DES 1989, 17.3). It abandoned the Britton-inspired dimensions of increasing awareness of audience and pur-pose (Britton et al 1975), despite Cox's assertion that 'linguistic forms cannot be corrected or assessed independently of their purpose' (DES 1989, 17.5). Instead, it introduced the term 'effectively' (one of the many judgemental rather than descriptive words of the revision) and the ques-tion-begging idea of 'standard' English (what about conveying meaning effectively in non-standard English as many major authors have done?)

When writing about the proposed attainment targets, the 1989 docu-ment distinguished between 'the composing aspects', covering 'language meaning, use and structure; the organisation, form and patterns of writ-ing', and the 'secretarial', 'concerning the pupil's competence in spelling and handwriting'. Of these abilities, 'the composing aspect is obviously by far the more important' (DES 1989, 17.26). In a significant reversal of emphasis, the 1993 proposals, focusing on 'the skills required' began:

> Particular attention is paid to the acquisition of standard English; grammatically correct expression, accurate spelling and conventional punctuation and an extensive vocabulary...Pupils should be taught that neat, legible handwriting is essential. Pupils should learn to organise their writing into paragraphs and complete texts. (NCC 1993, p.49.)

This shift had been foreshadowed in the way that the Secretary of State for Education called for the revision, stressing what he called 'the fundamental skills of the English Language' ('vital' apparently, 'for our economic growth and competitiveness'). The Chair of the NCC obediently provided a 'case for revising the order', where the criticism of the existing AT for Writing was that it 'does not offer a clear definition of basic writing skills, the grammatical knowledge pupils must master if they are to become effective writers, and the variety of ways in which competence in spelling can be developed' (NCC 1992, p.9). Such criticism rests on the dubious assumptions that there are separate 'basic writing skills' that we can identify, that 'extensive vocabulary' and 'accurate spelling' are discrete categories, and that 'mastering' grammatical 'knowledge' is a prerequisite of effective writing. In seeking to define quality and development in writing, the report repeatedly allows the mechanics to dominate. The reason is simple and deplorable. Everything is dominated by the need to ensure that the statements of attainment are 'amenable to standardized testing'. Because true quality in writing is not easily assessed in such ways, the emphasis is laid on those elements thought (though often wrongly) to be open to the 'clear definition' that is so much emphasised. 'Pupils should be taught' at Level 4 'to use commas in their own writing to represent pauses', at Level 5 to 'use apostrophes correctly'; at Level 7 they should be 'using semi-colons and colons', and by Level 9 they should be able 'to apply their knowledge of punctuation marks to their writing'. There are similar unreal distinctions about spelling. At Level 4, 'pupils should be taught to learn the spelling of complex, polysyllabic words which conform to regular patterns', at Level 5 to 'remember the visual pattern of letters in irregular spellings and spell inflectional suffixes correctly', at Level 6 to 'spell, in their own writing, longer or less familiar irregularly patterned words', and at Level 7 'learn how to spell specialist words in other subjects'.

When attempting to describe 'development' (1989) or 'progress' (1993), the two versions of National Curriculum English again display intriguing shifts of emphasis; the Cox version lays more emphasis on learning through the writing process, the NCC proposals on the written product that is to be 'conveyed' and 'improved'. Accordingly, instead of Cox's global statements of attainment, combining the 'composing' and 'secretarial', the 1993 proposals separate six strands: composition, forms of writing, grammar, punctuation, spelling and handwriting. In place of Cox's repeated phrase 'Pupils should be able to – ...' the Level-related programmes of the NCC 1993 version begin 'Pupils should be taught to – ...'.

Members of the Cox Committee were aware that their indicators of ability were not complete. Some vital marks of quality were omitted because they could not be fitted into the imposed curriculum structure. 'The best writing is vigorous, committed, honest and interesting. We have not included these qualities in our statements of attainment because they cannot be mapped on to levels' (DES 1989, 17.31). This frank acknowledgement of inability to define quality adequately was accompanied by awareness that development in writing is not neatly linear. 'Children do not learn particular features of written language once and for all at a particular stage. Development is recursive. This means that writing development must be defined in broad terms and cannot be measured solely by one-off tests at particular ages' (DES 1989, 17.25). This was given welcome acknowledgement in Dearing's report. Although he wrote of the desirability of 'a reliable and nationally uniform measure of a pupil's progress through his/her school years', he also emphasised how much 'cannot plausibly be sequenced into any linear scale' and that 'it is difficult to devise clear, unambiguous, hierarchical criteria except for simple or clearly defined tasks' (Dearing 1993, paras. 1.5 and 4.13).

One merit of Cox's programme of study was that it declined (or was unable) to play the ten-rung ladder game. It suggested that ability was manifested in a limited number of qualities that were not sequential but simply developed and grew more sophisticated in parallel. So, for example, the ability to 'write in a variety of forms for a range of purposes' is repeated with slight variations for all of Levels 5 to 10, eventually becoming 'Write, at an appropriate length, in a wide variety of forms with an assured sense of audience and purpose'. In a similar way, structure and organisation, or awareness of variations in vocabulary and syntax, or planning, drafting, revising and criticising, all recur at the six different levels. By contrast, the 1993 version of 'forms of writing' proposed unreal variations that are developmentally dubious: 'using formal language where an impersonal style is required' (Level 5), 'incorporating appropriate headings and other organisational devices' (Level 6), 'select and adapt language and content for demanding tasks' (Level 7), 'write in a wide range of forms, confidently using the structures, vocabulary and layout required'

(Level 8), 'write in a distinctive personal style' (Level 9), culminating in 'write confidently in a personal style showing the ability to enhance their writing through adapting form and presentation' (Level 10). The apparent precision is a sham; the phrases do not define separate steps in ability.

Conclusion

The impression of uncertainty and agnosticism created by this chapter may seem threatening or depressing. It needs to be added that amid the changing and conflicting views of those charged with their education, children do 'learn to write', they 'develop' as writers, their work reveals 'ability' – however shaky those terms may be when subjected to close analysis. As has been suggested, how we talk about ability in writing is influenced ideologically by whether we approach the subject from a 'top-down' or 'bottom-up' position. Government currently favours the top-down approach to policy, seeking some authoritative official view to which everyone should subscribe. Such a model assumes that it is possible to define the nature of writing ability in terms that are universally applicable. This ability (like abilities in talking and reading) is manifested quite unproblematically in pupils' performance; it is a quality inherent in their texts and capable of being objectively assessed. The weakness of this approach is that it has failed to learn from past experience just how complex are the concepts involved. Disputes over the form of the National Curriculum demonstrate that if we wait for accurate and agreed official definitions of writing ability or for reliable tests of quality, then we will wait for ever. We have to admit that our understanding of what happens in the minds of people when they are writing is still rudimentary. Simplistic notions about the writing process and dubious generalisations are dangerous when they are used to influence or even to dictate the curriculum of schools. The frank admissions of uncertainty in Cox's English order were infinitely preferable to what is called 'a clear definition of basic writing skills' which actually rests on shaky assumptions and ignores so much that we do know. All writing can serve a socialising purpose – even the notion of a personal 'voice' is culturally determined – but that does not necessarily imply a curriculum model that seeks to define arbitrarily what language features 'all' students at a given stage should know or be able to deploy.

Simplistic ideas are still more dangerous when underpinning programmes of testing. The DFE has run an expensive advertising campaign to suggest to parents that National Curriculum testing will give them important information about their children's progress. In fact, though, teachers report that it gives little or no help in defining ability in writing, in assessing pupils or in diagnosing their needs. The testing of writing is a highly political act. What precisely is to be tested, how, in what way and for what audience and purpose? The people who are in a position to answer these questions – whether politicians, administrators, assessment specialists, or writing theorists – exercise power over others. At the national level, the clearest and most helpful national picture of ability in writing that we have was given by the Assessment of Performance Unit, and the government might do well to reinstate such a body. By contrast, the notion that simple tests can be interpreted as 'proofs' that one school, teacher or region is more effective than another is both misguided and damaging to any who teach to such tests.

There is, however, another approach to this problem: the bottom-up model which acknowledges that notions of ability are constructed in the relationship between writer and reader, that the criteria are personal, individual and context specific. Wider agreement is reached by sharing individual perceptions of particular examples, as in the monitoring of GCSE coursework. This idea of ability is grounded in the classroom, not in the Department for Education. The success in literary competitions of children from some schools and teachers reinforces the commonsense view that teaching makes a significant difference. As Dearing said in his final recommendations, only teachers can directly improve educational standards. Writing is an interactive process. Children are highly influenced by situation and audience. They only produce their best work for teachers they trust and whose guidance they appreciate; their writing is significantly affected by what they have internalised about a teacher's view of 'good' work.

From their side of this interaction, effective English teachers know that they are reacting personally to their students' work; they are sceptical about the possibility of any helpful judgement being 'impartial', or 'objective'. Such teachers have learned over the years what it means to 'read' students' work, how to construct meaning which takes into account a relationship with the person who wrote it, the situation of the writing and what preceded it, and the need to respond in a way that develops that relationship. Understanding grows from familiarity with a body of work of different kinds produced and revised over a period of time. That is why most English teachers believe passionately in assessment by coursework rather than by stand-and-deliver tests. At the classroom level, they would say that any assessment of ability must be judged by the success with which it enables students themselves to reflect on the qualities of their own writing and to see how these can be developed. That depends much less on awarding grades and levels than on face-to-face discussions, during as well as after the writing, on identifying what can be rehandled and how, on building up portfolios of work, and on providing genuine, interested and responsive audiences. In the end, all depends on the quality of the individual encounter, and we should beware of over-generalising from the particular. It would be sensible to take to heart the conclusion of Alan Purves, reflecting on the lessons to be drawn from the massive international study of writing ability:

> We should beware of talking too facilely about concepts like writing performance or writing ability. They are task dependent and culture dependent as well. *We cannot say that someone is a better writer than someone else*. All we can say is at this particular time we think person A wrote a good composition on this topic. (Purves 1992, p.200, my italics.)

CHAPTER 5

The assessment of response to reading: developing a post-modern perspective

Introduction

In this chapter I want to argue that it is extraordinarily difficult to get very close to a person's response to what they read. Taken further, this assertion will lead to another: that it is extraordinarily difficult to make a very satisfactory job of assessing a person's ability in reading. What I aim to do is to examine some of the implications of this position, in relation to our current practices in assessing ability in reading, and then to make an attempt to redefine a basis for making more principled attempts to assess ability in reading, given that it is in certain important respects, impossible. My goal is not to lead towards a position of hopelessness or solipsism in relation to assessment, but rather to suggest that it is important to recognise the limitations in what we do, and to recognise that, even if we have come to act as if this were not the case, the assessment of reading remains fundamentally problematic. At the time of writing, the Dearing Review of the National Curriculum (1993) has suggested that there should be a moratorium on the development of new assessment procedures at national level, in order that teachers and pupils are spared further stress and disruption. This is understandable, but in many ways the timing of this moratorium is most unfortunate. There are many problems with current approaches to assessing reading, and I would argue that we should be actively investigating alternative approaches, and that teachers should be closely involved in developing these.

The structure of the chapter is as follows. I begin by attempting to develop the argument that it is difficult or impossible to assess response to reading directly. I then suggest six implications of this position. The general implication is that in assessing reading we need to take a post-modern perspective, and to put the emphasis back on the reader, rather than on the concept of reading comprehension, and I develop this point in two ways. One is by suggesting that we should attempt to investigate response through a reading interview; I suggest that through an interview we can focus on and place value upon what a person is choosing to read, and what they choose to say about their reading. I try to argue, through looking in detail at two readers, one avid reader who has much to say, and one very tentative reader who seems to have almost nothing to say, that a reading interview could provide evidence of reading which could be kept as a developing record of reading and response, and would be potentially much more valuable than a test result, or series of such results. I then go on to describe new thinking in the psychology of reading comprehension, and suggest that such research implies that instead of stressing the concept of *meaning* in assessing a reader's comprehension, it would be much more useful to attempt to teach, and to evaluate, the *strategies* which a reader brings to their reading. I argue that if the interview gives us access to the *what* of reading, an evaluation of readers' strategies leads us to a consideration of the *how*. Finally, I suggest that while these post-modern approaches to the assessment of reading might seem novel, they are in fact compatible with the goals of the National Curriculum, and also in harmony with innovative approaches to portfolio assessment which are being developed in other countries (for two accounts of these approaches, see Graves and Sunstein 1992, and Tierney, Carter and Desai 1991).

It is not possible to assess reading directly

So, back to the beginning. I want to suggest that it is not possible to get very close to a person's response to what they read. This problem is not a new one, but it has been thrown into sharper relief since 1988, and the introduction of a National Curriculum in England and Wales, in Scotland, and more recently in Northern Ireland. All these initiatives have required teachers to focus on the assessment of reading as something independent of other language areas. Until recently, English teachers have tended not to do this. In the examination systems at the end of the years of compulsory schooling, the tradition has increasingly been to eschew the comprehension tests of the 1950s, which grew out of a wartime need for rapid global assessments of the reading ability of thousands of recruits, and to assess reading as a part of 'English' or 'English Literature', and to assess a person's abilities in a unified way. This development was entirely reasonable, but in doing so, the problem of how one gains access to a person's actual response to reading was side-stepped.

Until recently, for example, teachers would naturally have claimed to be able to look at their pupils' response to reading, by pointing to the writing which offered evidence on their abilities in reading. In recent years, oral tasks have also become a part of formal assessment, including the assessment of response to reading, and, although teachers know that there are still many problems related to establishing reliability through moderation procedures, there has been a tendency to downplay any anxieties related to these problems, and a feeling that on balance it is worthwhile to have oracy as part of the assessed curriculum in English, because of its importance in the subject as a whole. When the different National Curriculum groups in the UK gave prominence to Speaking and Listening as separate components of the curriculum in English, most teachers were pleased, since this gave substance and legitimacy to the place of oracy as a fundamental part of English. It then seemed reasonably consistent to recognise the importance of reading, by making reading too a separate area of study and for assessment. After all, we have had reading tests for decades, and the Assessment of Performance Unit had reported separately on reading for nearly ten years over the period 1981–1991.

But consider for a moment what actually constitutes a person's response to reading. Can we see it? Can we measure it? Can we store it and replay it? Can we make it available in any direct way for further examination, moderation, discussion? We can see writing, and photocopy it. We can hear talk, and record it on tape, but in what sense can we gain access to reading? Reading involves the construction of meaning, and in this sense is an active process, but most of the activity is private. The eyes move, and they tell us that processing seems to be taking place, but not what the nature of that processing is. Electrical activity occurs in particular areas of the brain during reading, but we have no clear idea of what this activity betokens in terms of such factors as representation, comprehension or understanding. What is novel in the current assessment climate is that we have been required to consider the assessment of reading independently of the assessment of speaking and listening or of writing, and this has forced us to acknowledge that in important ways it is not possible to assess reading at all, except through substantial linguistic and psychological transformations; that is to say, through speaking or writing. There appear at first sight to be some exceptions to this general rule. For example, some multiple-choice comprehension questions do not require a person to write or speak: they require a response such as a tick, or a mouse-click on a computer, but even these do not permit us to get close to a reader's response, except in artificial and manufactured ways.

Young children and failing readers take reading tests, and because such tests are felt by those who set them to give some information, we ignore the problem that such tests do not actually get close to a personal response to reading. With young children, the most common way in which we attempt to assess reading is through listening to what they say. We ask children to read single words, to read a passage aloud, to talk about a story, or to retell a story. From this evidence, entirely understandably, we draw conclusions about their reading. But we need to remind ourselves that what we assess, first and foremost, is their speech.

We may justifiably claim that there is a correlation between what a child says and what that child has read, but the fact remains: it is speech which is the primary evidence, and, as all teachers know, what children say can be a poor correlate of reading comprehension. Some children seem able to read with fluency and good intonation, but are unable to offer a syllable of explanation about the meaning of the text they have read. Conversely, another child might read haltingly, with errors (or 'miscues') of omission, substitution or pronunciation, and with a monotonic evenness of tone which ignores the rules of sentence prosody, and seems to imply a total disregard for sentence or phrase boundaries. However, when questioned about the meaning of the passage, such a child might be lucid, intelligent and accurate, astonishing the listener with his or her grasp of the deep as well as the surface meaning of what was read. In this second case, we have evidence of comprehension, but again the primary evidence is speech. It is the reader's fluent speech which surprises us, and this fluent speech which leads us to conclude that the child is a fluent reader. The point is not that this is unreasonable, but rather that we sometimes neglect to acknowledge what the real evidence is upon which we are making our judgement about reading comprehension.

In the case of those who are not beginning readers or problem readers, the most common way of attempting to examine reading is through examining a person's writing. It is important, however, to acknowledge that here again, what readers make available to an observer through their writing is an edited and transformed version of their response. Rather like those reports of court cases on television, in which we see only an artist's impression of the scene, and hear a reporter's version of what took place, a person's written or spoken account of their reading must inevitably be an edited and transformed version of any initial response.

The problem is not simply that we cannot enter the reader's mind. There is rather, as in the court scene, a three-fold problem. First, any representation of 'what happened' has to be translated into another communicative medium, which will necessarily be partial, selective and edited, just as an artist's impression of a complex and changing scene is a selective and partial representation of the original. Second, the representation will inevitably be mediated by the reader's capacity to operate effectively in that medium, so it will inevitably be a poorer reflection, and it may be very much poorer. In other words, the artist may be a poor artist, or may be having an off day, or may have a limited understanding of what is taking place. Third, there is the uncertainty principle – you cannot elicit any response to reading without changing the nature of the processing of what is read. The task itself determines that response. In the court scene, a request to the artist to depict the defendant would lead to a different representation of the scene than that which the artist might have chosen to make if there had been no specific request. Equally, any attempt to probe response to reading is likely to bring about a new and different response to the text. For a question does not simply probe the reader's response, it prompts and directs that response, it both constructs and constrains it.

What are the implications of the fact that it is not possible to assess reading directly?

What I am arguing, therefore, is that we cannot really get close to assessing a person's response to reading without both missing a great deal and changing a great deal. It is not possible to assess what takes place in a person's mind when they read. Are visual images formed? Sometimes. Are partial meanings grasped and integrated? Certainly. Are individual words recognised, sentences boiled down into kernel propositions, and checks made on grammatical structure? Generally, yes. Are emotions stirred? Often. Is new information built upon old? Yes, and we assume that the manner in which this is done must be unique for every reader, since the scaffolding upon which the new information is built is unique for every reader. But how is all this accomplished? And what might we usefully say about this enormously complex parallel processing activity? We can, for example, talk about changes in visual memory and in semantic memory during reading, but to do so is really no more than to utilise metaphors which explain or predict aspects of a reader's response. Psychologists often use the term 'representation' to refer to what a reader's mind produces while reading, but upon closer analysis this word seems to be used as a general term which hides as much as it reveals. In fact, while the term is used widely, psychologists are extremely cautious in making any claim to know much about what the nature of this 'representation' is.

Psychologists understandably attempt to isolate one aspect of reading at a time for investigation, but we need to remind ourselves that a reader's response seems to occur in a number of domains: affective, verbal and visual. By contrast, what is usually sought when as teachers we attempt to investigate a person's response is primarily verbal, and an emphasis on the verbal therefore not only constrains and changes that aspect of the response, it is also likely to constrain, change, marginalise or ignore altogether other aspects of the response.

To attempt to assess response to reading is therefore to change and determine the nature of the reading activity. Any attempt to assess response will bring about a change in some or all of the following: (a) the attentional and affective processes which are part of reading, (b) the processes of comprehension, of integrating meaning and relating new input to previous knowledge, and (c) the processes related to organising and producing the response, in written, spoken, or non-discourse form.

What are the implications of all this, for rethinking how we consider ability in reading? Here are six:

1. We need to be more aware of the inaccessibility of reading processes.

2. If we wish to assess reading as a separate language area, we need to consider ways of developing assessment procedures which attempt to value individual response, and which attempt to get close to that response.

3. We need to be more aware of the inevitable intrusiveness of assessment in relation to reading and the reading process, and that any method of evoking or making assessable a reader's response necessarily changes that response.

4. We need therefore to become even more aware of and thoughtful about the tasks we set and approaches we adopt in seeking to find out about response to reading.

5. We need to be aware of the extent to which, when we wish to assess ability in reading, we are likely to be assessing speaking or writing as well.

6. We need to be aware that responding in writing to what has been read requires a double transformation, from reading response, into verbal discourse, and then into written form, and in the light of this we should consider methods of eliciting responses to reading which do not disadvantage those who are not fluent writers.

What would it be to reconsider how we look at ability in reading in the light of these implications? What would it be to begin with a blank sheet of paper? Consider for a moment why humans engage in reading in the first place. Why do we have print? Why do adults choose to read? Why do school students read? Some of the most common explanations for why school students read are: to engage in the transactions of everyday life, for enjoyment, to pass examinations. These purposes encompass many of the goals of English teaching, but such formulations are essentially utilitarian. If we are seeking a more complete expression of why reading is important, we could do worse than turn to the words of Flaubert, who articulated better than most the profoundly idealistic part of our teacherly intentions with respect to reading:

Do not read, as children do, to amuse yourself, or like the ambitious, for the purpose of instruction. No, read in order to live. (Gustave Flaubert, letter to Mlle de Chantepie, June, 1957.)

When we begin from this point, and attempt to reconsider what it might be to reflect on ability in reading, we find ourselves redefining assessment. Instead of seeing assessment as a set of practices which are essentially technical, to do with gradually improving a set of reading test instruments, and gradually 'improving' a set of readers, we are forced to reconsider the whole reading process, and the psychological and social imperatives which underpin it. Perhaps surprisingly, it is in acknowledging the importance of Flaubert's nineteenth-century perspective that we are impelled to move to a post-modern view of assessment. This is because it is from within the post-modern perspective that we need to begin with a consideration of the reader rather than the assessment task, and with an acknowledgement that assessing ability in reading is not a value-free exercise, but an activity which is socially and culturally located. As Peter Johnston put it (1993), 'assessment has to do with how we know and represent ourselves and each other as literate individuals and as a literate society.' And just as post-modern currents have redefined literary theory, so similar currents are now redefining assessment theory.

The main consequence of a post-modern perspective on reading is a recognition that our very definitions of ability and assessment are based upon, and give status to, certain values and value systems. 'Ability', therefore, is not an absolute; it is a cultural artefact, and the matter of its definition is far from trivial, for the definition of 'ability' has an important function, namely to determine social and cultural status in the domain of literacy. Its definition is not simply a matter of academic debate, but also one of social control and power. If we define ability in reading in terms of scores on National Curriculum tests, we give social power to the test and to those who perform well on it. Conversely, if we define ability in terms which tests do not measure, and which begin with readers, or with the professional wisdom and understanding of teachers, we privilege those perspectives and give social power to those groups. One point which emerges from this analysis is that the current tension which exists between teacher assessment and assessment through national tests is not simply a matter of workload or test administration detail; it is a fundamental issue relating to control and power over the definitions of literacy in our society.

At this point the reader might reasonably ask whether a post-modern analysis should not apply to all areas of assessing ability in English. My answer would be that it should, but I would also suggest that there are specific reasons why the assessment of reading has come to the forefront of public attention in recent years. There is an innate conservatism built into reading assessment, since it is part of the publishing industry, and it therefore has the stability (or inertia) which is related to its having produced hundreds of tests over a period of years, with a concomitant tendency towards a technical and utilitarian model of theory. Despite this conservatism, however, there are two specific reasons why reading assessment has found itself being redefined during the past decade. First, the field of reading has become the site for battles over the literary canon, battles which are focussed around the issues of social and cultural power, and if decisions over what is to be read are matters of cultural practice and belief which need to be anatomised and deconstructed, so too are decisions about how we examine and give value to the responses which people make to those printed texts. Second, definitions of the term literacy itself are matters which have thrust themselves into the political arena. Such definitions bestow power within cultures, and have serious implications, for example by privileging technological literacy, or by positing a causal link between illiteracy and crime. Reading, therefore, tends to find itself discussed as a political and public issue ahead of oracy and writing, although recent debates about standard spoken and written English have brought these too into the area of public debate.

Put another way, what I am saying is that the issue of construct validity in assessing ability in reading is something which we have tended to ignore, but it is an issue which has come increasingly to the fore. Construct validity is a measure of the extent to which what we choose to measure really does relate fundamentally to the underlying construct, in this case reading. In the 1990s we are less clear about what counts as construct validity in reading for one very simple reason: we are problematising the construct.

Having attempted to identify some of the principles upon which the assessment of ability in reading should be based, it is my intention in the remainder of this chapter to attempt to apply these principles in two ways. First, I want to put an emphasis on the reader, and to ask in what ways and to what extent we can reconsider ability in reading in relation to what readers have to say about what they read, through a reading interview. Second, I want to consider the implications of new perspectives in psychology for our understanding of reading comprehension, in terms of how we define it, how we measure it, and how we teach it, and I shall attempt to connect this discussion to the assessment of reading within the National Curriculum.

The reading interview

Are there ways in which we can attempt, legitimately and validly, to get close to a person's response to reading? In order to begin to answer this question, I want to suggest that we consider transcripts of two readers who were recorded by their teacher as they talked with her about what they had read and why they chose to read it. Naturally, we must begin by acknowledging that what we are looking at is speech written down, and that the teacher's questions will have helped to shape the response. Nevertheless, the teacher did know these children well, the interviews were voluntary, and the questions were carefully considered and intended to avoid direct prompting, so far as was possible. Again, while it would be inappropriate to claim that we are close to examining directly what people think and feel when they read, I would want to suggest that in listening to Emma's and Brett's reflections on their reading, we can learn something about response to reading, and about ability in reading, which we could not learn from a test. At the time of these interviews, Brett was twelve, and Emma was fourteen. The interviews were conducted informally, in the library of a Nottinghamshire school, by Mary Bailey (1993) and I am grateful to her for letting me use them. The interviews were quite extensive, and what is reproduced below is only a part of what was recorded. What is particularly important about these interviews is that they begin with much more global questions than those which we would normally ask.

The sort of evidence a reading interview might offer of the reader's response to reading is described by Protherough in his excellent *Developing a Response to Fiction* (1983). Protherough suggested a number of helpful general categories of response, based upon extensive observations of a group of children by their teachers in the Hull area. He suggested five main categories, and proposed that they might be viewed hierarchically, as indicative of an increasing distancing of perception on the part of the reader. In other books, Protherough has suggested alternative approaches to categorising response, but I find those in this book especially useful. The categories, together with a brief example of each, are as follows:

1. *Projection into character* – 'I put myself in the person's place I am

reading about.' (girl, 13).

2. *Projection into situation* – 'I feel as though I am there, witnessing the events. I am the characters' friend.' (boy, 13).

3. *Associating between book and reader* – 'When I read, the things which pass through my mind are similar experiences of my own.' (girl, 13).

4. *The distanced viewer* – 'I feel differently for the characters: if they are unhappy I pity them, if they are mean I hate them.' (girl, 14).

5. *Detached evaluation* – 'When I read a book, the things that go through my mind are whether I can understand the characters, the way in which they act and why they act in a certain way.' (girl, 17).

It is, of course, no simple matter to decide on the reader's 'distance of perception', but here I want to suggest not so much that Protherough's approach is easy or especially reliable, but rather that it is in principle both valid and worthwhile, in that it relates usefully to a consideration of the discourse of personal response which children themselves choose to adopt.

In considering this fairly substantial section of the interview with Emma, I would suggest that we can see all of Protherough's categories, and more. I will go on to suggest that this type of evidence, difficult though it is to obtain, can take us closer to the immediacy of a reader's response than other assessment procedures, and that in doing so it can offer us a less transformed and constrained perspective on a reader's abilities than that which a direct probing of a person's 'critical' response to texts might elicit.

Emma (aged 14)

Teacher: Can you tell me how many books you've read in the last month, approximately?

Emma: About...probably twenty or more.

Teacher: Probably twenty or more. Now is that a typical amount for you to read in a month?

Emma: Yes.

Teacher: Now could you just, obviously you're not going to be able to remember all of those, just off the top of your head without writing them down, but could you tell me some of the titles that you remember from the last month?

Emma: Yes. Well, I've got several books of my own, new books. There was two, um, Sherlock Holmes books: The Adventures of Sherlock Holmes and, er, The Sign of Four, by Conan, er. Um, and then there was a book by Francine Pascale, The Sweet Valley Saga. Um, another book by Francine Pascale, Regina's Legacy. Then I've got a big thick, that, it's called The Dark is Rising Sequence, by Susan Cooper, and that's good. And then several other sort of Sweet Dreams books that I read. They're very easy reading. And also from the library I got a JFK folder out, 'cause I've just seen the film and so I got the file out of the library and just had a look, basically, at the layout of what happened [first off?] 'cause I'm not interested in that kind of thing.

Teacher: Right. Now all of those books that you read you finished, you read from beginning to end, did you?

Emma: Yes.

Teacher: Right. Do you ever give up a book for any reason?

Emma: No.

Teacher: No. Why's that?

Emma: 'Cause even if it's boring it's got, I mean, there must be a reason why they've carried on writing it.

Teacher: Right.

Emma: So, like, White Peak Farm. I mean everybody was going on how boring that was, but I thought it was quite interesting.

Teacher: Right. Have you ever got to the end of the book and thinking, oh well, that wasn't really worth it?

Emma: Not really, no.

Teacher: Right. What do you get out of reading then? I mean, obviously you are a very keen reader and you know that you read an exceptionally high number of books, certainly compared to other people in the class. Why do you think that is, that you do that? What do you get out of reading so much?

Emma: Well I think it's, I mean, like you pick up new words from books and as well you can have your own vision of what's happening. Whereas on television it's all made for you.

Teacher: Right.

Emma: It's like exercising your imagination.

Teacher: Right.

Emma: So...I just enjoy it really.

Emma is not an academic high flyer, but she is the kind of pupil many English teachers would dream of having in their class. First, she is an avid reader, and this is an important part of what we learn about her reading. In England, some teachers might be inclined to react to finding that a person is an avid reader with the question, 'But what do they read, and is it worthwhile or is it rubbish?' This is understandable, but it may also be an

unhelpfully elitist response. At an Anglo-Scandinavian reading conference which I attended, there was astonishment among the Danish and
Finnish delegates when a UK presenter referred to the fact that some
British children were reading 'rubbish'. The Scandinavians found the use
of this term surprising, and said that it would be unheard of in their countries to dismiss the fact that children were motivated enough to read by
using such a derogatory term. They hinted that if the British were not so
obsessed with elitism and intellectual snobbery, their pupils might read
more widely and reading standards would improve, without any threat to
the fabric of the nation's culture! They had a point. In a recent international study of reading standards, the Finns were found to have the highest reading standards in the world.

As well as being an avid reader, Emma offers many evaluative judgements about what she reads. She describes Francine Pascale as 'easy reading', which suggests an awareness of relative difficulty, an ability to place
books on a personal continuum of complexity. She uses terms which most
children use, such as 'boring' and 'interesting', but goes beyond these,
and hints at quite a sophisticated awareness of an author's intentions,
'Cause even if it's boring it's got, I mean, there must be a reason why
they've carried on writing it.' Emma is also aware of what she gains from
her reading: enjoyment, developing vocabulary, and a stimulation of the
imagination.

In a later part of the interview, the teacher asks Emma how much television she watches. Without any direct prompting, Emma volunteers that
she cannot watch television straight after finishing a book, and this leads
into a fascinating account of her feelings, which covers all five of
Protherough's levels, and incidentally reveals how valuable it can be to
read books which some teachers might dismiss as 'rubbish'.

Emma: If I've finished a book then I can't watch the telly straight after
          I've read the book, because everything has to sink in.
Teacher: Right.
Emma: I sometimes just lie down and just think about what's happened,
          you know, like, it's like you've watched telly, but it just like
          sinks in after I've read it.
Teacher: Right. When you say you like to think about a book and let it
          sink in, what sort of things do you think about? What goes
          through your mind when you're letting a book sink in?
Emma: Well, I, if it's a murder book, I think about why they did it, you
          know, what I would have done in their position, and things like
          that. I mean, I know it sounds silly, but I just try and put myself
          in the other people's points of view. Like, what it would be like

to be on the run, you know. And that sort of thing.

Teacher: That's not silly at all. That's interesting. So do you quite often put yourself in other people's positions when you're reading?

Emma: Yes, I like to try to, yes.

Teacher: Mm. Does, um, this will be a bit of an unusual question, but when you're not reading, you know, when you're just going about your ordinary life, does anything ever remind you of books that you've read? Do you ever think about books that you've read after you've read them, you know, some time after you've read them?

Emma: Yes. I mean, like this newspaper business. In the Sweet Valley High books there's a school newspaper and it's an American thing, a school newspaper, and that reminded me quite a lot of this, you know. That's why I was quite keen to get into it.

Teacher: Yes. Right. Um, would you, again this is going to be a bit of a weird question, would you say that ever, that reading books helps you to think about your life in any way?

Emma: Yes and no, because sometimes it, in a book, if, like the Sweet Valley High books, there's one person in the Sweet Valley High that I'd like to be like. But the thing is, if I was like her then my school work would go down and I wouldn't really be very good at home. You know, I'd be always making excuses, but like, it does help me some ways because like it's like if she does something in one situation it makes me think about what I'd do in that situation. But like, if she, if she tries to get out of something that you, I know that I'd be in trouble for, you know like on one of the books she's making phone calls to people. Um, you know, I'd never do that, but in some ways it makes you think about what would happen if you did make a phone call to somebody. You know, so...

Teacher: So does that mean that you don't have to do it because you can just imagine it?

Emma: You don't have, the thing is it like puts ideas into your head.

Teacher: Mm.

Emma: Some of the books, um, they're very unrealistic. You know, it's things that wouldn't happen. I mean like in one of the books all on the same day she goes to a party, she drives a motorbike which she's promised her parents she'd never ride again, she falls off it and she's in a coma. You know. And it all happens in one day and that wouldn't happen. I mean, maybe she'd get on the motorbike and ride it and maybe she would be in an accident, but the way it's told, it's just unrealistic, you know. So sometimes, things like that you can tell that it wouldn't really happen.

What Emma is sharing with her teacher at the beginning of this section is perhaps one of the most important, but also one of the most inexpressible parts of our response to reading. Some minutes into the interview, and alone with a teacher she trusts, Emma speaks of the time when she needs to be apart with her feelings, so that a book can 'sink in'. This is the time when a reader just wants to be alone, to experience further the emotions the book evokes, and to take time to reflect on how the world in the book resonates with her own world. It is to help others to experience these moments that people become teachers of English, and yet because it is so difficult to identify, still less to capture, such responses, I want to suggest that in assessing response we tend to focus on other, much less important, but more accessible areas.

Emma also reveals that she projects into character ('I just try and put myself in the other people's points of view') and into situation ('Like, what it would be like to be on the run, you know'). She makes an association between a book and her own experiences by comparing her school work on a class newspaper with the school newspaper in Sweet Valley High ('I mean, like this newspaper business. In the Sweet Valley High books there's a school newspaper and it's an American thing, a school newspaper, and that reminded me quite a lot of this, you know'). However, this projection is not only distanced, it includes an awareness that Emma herself would not act in the way the character did ('Um, you know, I'd never do that, but in some ways it makes you think about what would happen if you did make a phone call to somebody'). Finally, Emma shows clearly the detached evaluation of Protherough's fifth stage, when she comments on the compressed action of the party in which events which could occur independently combine to take place within a fictional frame which is too small to hold them.

What I am suggesting here, therefore, is that a reading interview can offer a principled basis for assessing ability in reading, that it can be much less intrusive than other approaches to prompting response, and that it can be related to indices of development in maturity of response.

Let us now listen in on part of the interview with Brett, and consider to what extent a conversation with a very different type of reader might provide useful evidence for making judgements about response to reading and ability in reading. We shall again consider Protherough's categories, and suggest that they remain useful, but might perhaps be developed to accommodate Brett's less developed responses. Protherough referred to readers who had little to say about their reading, and wrote of those who 'either did not understand questions about how they read, or who were not willing to respond to them' (Protherough 1983, p.21). Some of the children on whom he reported said simply, 'I just read it, that's all' or 'If it's interesting I keep reading it and if it's boring I stop.' He suggested that such children are ones for whom reading is perhaps an 'automatic decoding process', and described such readers as those on whom 'fiction makes little impact, or none that the reader is prepared to acknowledge'. In reading Brett's transcript, we might be tempted to place Brett in this 'little impact' category, but I wish to suggest that he reveals a good deal about his response to reading.

Brett (aged 12)

Teacher: Right. Can you tell me again how many books you read in the last four weeks.

Brett: Two.

Teacher: Right. Which books were they?

Brett: The Twits and Matilda.

Teacher: Right. And can you remember who wrote those?

Brett: Yes. Roald Dahl.

Teacher: Right. Why do you like those two?

Brett: Because they're funny.

Teacher: Have you read them before?

Brett: Yes.

Teacher: How many times would you say you'd read them altogether?

Brett: Twice.

Teacher: You've read them both twice.

Teacher: Okay. Who would you say was your favourite author?

Brett: Roald Dahl.

Teacher: Roald Dahl. Now what, those two books that you mentioned by him, why do you like those so much? You said they're funny, but can you say a bit more about why you like them?

Brett: No.

Teacher: No? What sort of things do you think about when you're reading them?

Brett: Nothing.

Teacher: Nothing? You just enjoy the story do you?

Brett: Yes.

Teacher: Okay. And do you usually read them all in one go?

Brett: No.

Teacher: Right. What would you say makes a good book?

Brett: When it's funny.

Teacher: Right. And what would you say is funny? What sort of things do you think are funny? Can you say? That's a difficult question.

Brett: No.

Teacher: No idea?

Brett: No.

Teacher: Okay. Right. What other things do you read? Do you read comics?

Brett: Yes.

Teacher: Which?

Brett: Um, Look-In and Fast Forward.

Teacher: Right. Why do you like them?

Brett: 'Cause they're about a lot of interesting things.

Teacher: Like what?

Brett: Cars and games and stuff.

Teacher: Right.

Brett: And trains.

Teacher: Cars, games, trains. Do you buy those magazines or look at somebody else's or...

Brett: I buy them.

Teacher: Right. Um, do you read any newspapers at home?

Brett: No.

Teacher: So is there anything else that you read that other people have at home that you pick up and read sometimes?

Brett: No.

Teacher: Right. Can I ask you about television? What's your favourite television programme?

Brett: Neighbours.

Teacher: Right. Why do you like that?

Brett: Um. I don't know.

Teacher: Do you watch it every day?

Brett: No. Not always every day. Most days.

Teacher: Okay. What about other things that you do in your time? Have you got any other hobbies?

Brett: Yes. I play the organ.

Teacher: Right. How often do you do that?

Brett: Every night.

Teacher: Right. How long do you spend on doing that?

Brett: Well, some nights I spend quarter of an hour or something like that. Some nights I spend an hour and a half.

Teacher: Right. So that uses up quite a lot of your time.

Brett: Yes.

Perhaps Brett is not a great communicator. Perhaps he was shy or embarrassed at the time of the interview. Perhaps he is someone who would be classed as a poor reader by a standardised test. Whatever the reasons, and despite gentle prompting, he only had a limited amount to say about his reading. But although Brett was tentative, and his most frequent response to a question was 'No', we nevertheless learn a great deal about Brett's reading from the interview:

- He reads voluntarily, and in his own time.
- He is clear about why he likes the books he reads: 'because they're funny' and 'cause they're about interesting things'.
- He rereads books he likes.
- He has a favourite author, and can name him.
- He reads comics.
- He is prepared to spend money on his reading.

Brett is a reader, and this is important. What he has to say is limited, but the interview gave him opportunities to tell his teacher a good deal that she did not know before, and which, I would argue, might form a valuable contribution to any records which were kept in his school about his reading. Equally, I would suggest that what we learn about Emma's reading, and her feelings in relation to that reading, is pure gold. As teachers, we would be delighted to learn about those details of her inner world which Emma chooses to share, and yet how rarely do we have opportunities to offer our pupils a chance to tell us about such things?

The question to put, then, is this: should we be rethinking the assessment of reading, in order to accommodate the type of perspective on response which a reading interview can provide? I would argue that we should. It would, of course, be irresponsible for any lecturer in education to suggest that teachers should conduct regular interviews such as this with every child whom they teach, particularly in the current climate. It would place an enormous burden on teachers if it were suggested that such interviews should be conducted, even if interviews were to be fixed up no more than once per year. But suppose the assessment climate changed, and that there were to be no National Curriculum assessment; or suppose that instead of Standard Assessment Tasks, we were required to adopt an assessment system that began with the child rather than with the test? Would it not then be essential that we should have considered the most valuable ways of rethinking assessment?

As mentioned at the beginning of this chapter, the National Curriculum has recently been reviewed (Dearing 1993), and we have been told that in order to provide stability and to reduce the load on teachers, assessment procedures are to remain essentially unchanged for the time being. This is understandable, and Dearing's motives in relation to reducing stress on pupils and teachers are laudable, but while teachers need short-term pragmatic strategies for coping with assessment, I would suggest that it is absolutely essential to consider what assessment procedures should be proposed if educators, rather than the government, had the power to determine what was to be done. It would be unfortunate if we were to fail to explore alternatives to current assessment procedures, and if we were to leave a vacuum in terms of suggesting and exploring alternative theories and practices.

Rethinking reading comprehension

Assessment rarely stands still, and it certainly has not been standing still in other countries. At the same time as in England and Wales the government required schools to reduce the amount of coursework which could be included in assessment, other English-speaking countries have been doing the opposite, and have implemented regional and national projects to develop portfolio assessment procedures, which collect examples of pupils' work and include these in the assessment process.

Over the past twenty years, debates over standards of literacy in the USA have been at least as heated as those in the UK (see Stedman and Kaestle 1987, for a review), and the testing industry has played an influential part in the debates. More recently, however, it is clear that, in some areas at least, a type of testing ennui has set in. Colleagues in the US have become more and more dissatisfied with the type of information provided by standardised tests, for while tests may provide information which relates to debates on standards, they tend to provide very little useful information for the key person who needs it – the class teacher. In fact, the reverse is the case. If children find tests upsetting and demotivating, and if they feel they have little or no power to improve in the subject being tested, then testing is directly counter-productive. But teachers are not the only ones who have joined in a growing rebellion against traditional tests. Reading researchers, many of whom have worked for over twenty years with traditional tests, have come to reject them, and are seeking new alternatives.

How has this come about, and what alternatives are being proposed? To begin to answer this question, it is worth taking a step back, and considering not simply reading tests, but the construct which many reading tests are supposed to measure, namely reading comprehension. A recent review of research in reading comprehension (Dole et al 1991) in the *Review of Educational Research,* which is generally considered a fairly traditional journal within its native US, has been very influential in advancing the debate about how ability in reading is defined and measured. The paper, which was written by some of the most distinguished reading researchers in the US, is fairly dismissive of what have been called 'assembly-line' models of reading comprehension, which date back to the 1950s, and which view reading as a set of sub-skills. Such models would seek to describe readers' abilities in terms of comprehension sub-skills such as finding the main points in a passage, predicting outcomes, drawing conclusions, and so on, which, it was thought, could be tested, developed and mastered independently. Dole points out that there are many problems with such models, in particular the difficulty of determining what precisely constitutes a 'sub-skill', and subsequently identifying reliably the sub-skills in which a person is strong or weak.

Reading does not occur in the absence of a text, and the problem for sub-skills models is that readers behave like experts when they are handling familiar text, and like novices when they are handling unfamiliar text. Readers perform well on a 'sub-skill' when they understand a passage, but poorly when they do not. So ability in reading is not constant; it is context-related. Unfortunately, most reading curricula, including that in the latest National Curriculum for England and Wales (NCC 1993), find it nearly impossible to avoid adopting something very close to the 'sub-skills' paradigm, and to relate performance on 'sub-skills' to age levels. There were signs in some early documents produced in relation to assessment in English in England and Wales that it was recognised that variations in text difficulty posed problems for hierarchical models of reading comprehension. For example, in the Cox Report (DES 1989), the following point was offered as one of the principles which should guide subsequent approaches to assessment:

> ...since the assessment of language competence is dependent upon the task – and context (that is, a child may show different levels of performance in the same language area when undertaking tasks of different kinds or set in different contexts), the widest practicable range of types of tasks and settings should be used, including where appropriate the unfamiliar as well as the familiar. (Section 14.12.)

This principle is incompatible with statements of attainment such as 'Pupils should be able to talk about the main topic in a non-fiction text', which is taken from the 1993 revision of the document English in the National Curriculum (Statements of Attainment for Reading, Key Stage 1, Level 1; NCC 1993, p.29). To be able to 'talk about the main topic in a non-fiction text' is not a level-related 'skill'. If the text is 'Conker', by Barrie Watts, then that task is one which many pupils at Level 1 could tackle. If, however, the text is a rather different book on trees, J.G. Fraser's 'The Golden Bough' (which opens with the extraordinary sentence 'Who does not know Turner's picture of the Golden Bough?'), then the task itself is much more challenging. To be fair to the drafters of the 1993 curriculum document, however, one should note that reference to increasing text difficulty is woven into some of the statements of attainment (for example, 'Pupils should be able to explain in clear detail the meaning of complex sections of literary or non-literary texts'; Level 8), but the general point still stands: defining attainment in terms of 'sub-skills' is unreliable, and is not trusted by experts in reading assessment.

One final point should perhaps be made about the reading comprehension 'sub-skills' debate, and this is that while supposed 'sub-skills' may have little substance in terms of test validity and reliability, discourse related to what are termed reading *strategies* may have much more utility in terms of the reading curriculum. Dole and her co-authors point out that while the term 'skills' implies a passive, automatic and low-level psychological process, 'strategy' implies an active, deliberate and cognitively sophisticated approach to reading, which is under the conscious control of the reader. So to talk about reading strategies, and to teach them, or to teach pupils to be aware of them, is very worthwhile. It can give readers more power over their reading, and lead to the sort of 'active interrogation of the text' which was advocated in the Bullock Report, twenty years ago (DES 1975).

So what strategies does research suggest that we should teach, and do these provide a useful basis for extending our analysis of what one might attempt to assess in reading? The answer is most certainly affirmative, and the strategies provide a classroom basis for monitoring reading development which would complement the type of data available from a reading interview. Dole (1991, pp.243–249) suggests that the following strategies are the ones which research has shown can be effectively taught:

(a) Determining importance (identifying the main point, gist, or theme)
(b) Summarizing (involving synthesis and composition)
(c) Drawing inferences
(d) Generating questions
(e) Monitoring comprehension.

This list of strategies might seem remarkably similar to lists of sub-skills of the type I have been dismissing. What is important here is to recognise that Dole's strategies are reading *behaviours,* which we can teach and observe. They are processes, but what is crucial is that they are observable processes. Sub-skills are internal, automated processes, which are not observable. Another important point to emphasise is that evaluating a reader's use of reading strategies does not imply that a reader is searching for a single, agreed interpretation. If what is valued is the *process* of applying a certain strategy, interpretation remains open, and alternative interpretations are valued and accepted.

What, then are these strategies? It is worth offering a brief comment on each one. In each case, it is not the meaning which the reader arrives at which is the focus, but the active process of striving after that meaning which is what we are concerned with. The glosses are mine, but I have attempted to summarise the points from Dole's paper:

(a) **Identifying the most important information** in a passage is not the same thing as summarizing it. Identifying the most important information can be difficult, especially if the text structure gives few clues. Importance can be a relative rather than an absolute matter, however, and this means that strategies for identifying important information should be brought out, discussed and examined in relation to a variety of texts.

(b) **Summarizing information** is much more difficult than simply identifying what is important, since summarizing requires synthesising information – bringing together, condensing, simplifying – as well as composing, producing a written version.

(c) All reading requires the reader to **draw inferences**, but more experienced readers do this more fully and more expertly than less experienced readers. What is needed in terms of reading development is for the process of drawing inferences to be shared and made explicit, through examples and discussion, so that readers can learn precisely how others make use of the information within a text in order to read between the lines.

(d) **Generating questions in relation to texts** gives a helpful indication of close reading. Generating and sharing one's own questions can often involve closer reading than answering questions set by others, and it is often the first step in reading for research purposes.

(e) Closely related to the process of generating questions is that of **monitoring one's own comprehension.** One problem faced by readers using unfamiliar material is that of deciding whether or not they are understanding what is being read. Monitoring comprehension can involve identifying which parts of a passage are understood and which are not; this can be helpful, especially if others find problems with different sections. It is clearly important for pupils to be aware of how much they are understanding, and to be aware of how they deal with difficulties.

These reading strategies, therefore, are not 'sub-skills'. They are not low-level automated processes, but rather they are approaches to texts which are consciously regulated and actively applied. These strategies are ones which tend to be used by skilled readers, and tend not to be used by unskilled readers, and they can be taught. Having said this, however, we must repeat what has been stressed already, which is that we all behave as unskilled readers in certain circumstances. So we do not 'possess' these strategies in the sense that, once internalised, they are applied inevitably in all reading situations. Nevertheless, I would want to argue that in assessing reading we should begin to make the attempt to incorporate the assessment of the reader's ability to use these five strategies, for the following reason: the more constructive view of reading implied in emphasising reading *strategies* rather than reading comprehension is enormously important. It characterises reading as active, and places a value, not on *comprehension* alone, but on the student's ability to construct personal meanings from what is read.

To teach, and to attempt to assess, a reader's use of active comprehension strategies is not easy. First, for it to be of any use, the teaching would need to be contextualised rather than decontextualised. In other words, the assessment of a reader's use of reading strategies would not be based around passages arbitrarily selected by an examination board. It would focus on texts selected by the student and related to an authentic reading purpose, one which had some meaning and relevance for the student. It would focus on reading for a purpose, and such reading might be related to literary texts or to seeking information from reference sources. Second, in order to be in a position to assess a reader's use of strategies, a teacher would need to monitor and assess reading in action. This task would be at least as difficult as monitoring speaking and listening in the classroom, and in some respects would be more difficult. Assessment through traditional tests would yield very little information about the processes of active making of meaning, which, I am arguing, are at least as worthy of investigation than the products of that reading. Or, to put the matter another way, what I am suggesting is that it is the process itself which becomes the product, in the sense that it is an account of the process which one is seeking to capture, and that account becomes the 'product', the evidence which is retained for future reference, and which then becomes integrated as part of an assessment procedure.

In this respect, it might be useful to attempt to move away from a dichotomy which has come to permeate our views of reading in school, namely that reading literature is a subjective and personal activity, while reading for information is essentially an objective and utilitarian activity. If our understanding of reading is to take on a post-modern perspective, then we need perhaps to acknowledge that such a perspective should be applied equally to all texts. In order to accommodate a post-modern viewpoint, the teaching of literature needs to develop beyond the search for what has been called a 'collective subjectivity', arrived at through analyses of plot, character and language. If it is truly the case that the authority of the reader is to be more respected, and the authority of the author diminished, then it is appropriate to give less attention in assessment procedures to 'understanding', and more to valuing the processes through which a reader arrives at that understanding. But equally, in considering reading for information, there is a need for a post-modern perspective, in which we place less value on 'comprehension', and more on the processes of research and enquiry, on the reader's willingness and ability to explore texts, to compare versions of reality, and to problematise in what is read the concepts of 'fact' and 'truth'.

Although we may not have realised it fifteen years ago, it was precisely this opening up of texts to enquiry and exploration that Eric Lunzer and Keith Gardner were attempting to encourage through the Effective Use of Reading project (Lunzer and Gardner 1979), and its successor, the project on Reading for Learning in the Secondary School (Lunzer and Gardner 1984). Their proposals, and the Directed Activities Related to Texts (DARTs) which accompanied them, were not so much improvements on comprehension exercises as radical alternatives to them, designed not only to encourage active approaches to reading, but to redefine the relationship between author, reader and text. At the time of its publication, Lunzer's work was interpreted by some commentators as utilitarian and derived from Skinnerian behaviouristic principles. They could not have been more wrong. Instead of a transmissional view of learning, the projects were in fact applying post-modern principles to reading, and these principles applied to fiction and non-fiction alike. The DARTs activities were based on small group discussions focussed around such things as deletions from texts, manipulations of text structure, the critical reading of diagrams and tables, and so on. All of these activities tended to place the reader alongside the author as meaning maker, rather than to position the reader as a passive recipient of knowledge transmitted from the author. Lunzer's work remains enormously important, in that, some years ahead of its time, it encouraged the notion that texts are an archaeological site for exploring meaning, rather than a cemetery from which meaning is exhumed.

Some conclusions

I want to suggest, then, that it would be possible to take a post-modern view of what is important in reading, and to make it a fundamental part of both the teaching and assessment. There are problems, but they can be dealt with, provided that there is a will to overcome them. I have suggested that the National Curriculum in England and Wales currently presents an unworkable model of assessment. Nevertheless, it is the one teachers in these countries have to work with, and even if the assessment procedures are problematic, the National Curriculum remains a valuable guide to what readers need to be able to do. I would suggest that nearly all the statements of attainment describe behaviours which relate to important areas of reading and reading development. Where the curriculum is unworkable is in relation to Levels and Key Stages, not in terms of overall objectives. If teachers were permitted to move towards a portfolio assessment system, within which evidence of reading activity, reading interviews, reading conversations and reading strategies could be stored and retained, and if this evidence included details of the nature and variety of texts encountered, most of the problems associated with national curriculum levels of attainment would evaporate. What an assessment system requires is evidence of what has been achieved, and a portfolio system would provide this.

Teachers of English in England and Wales have proved themselves to be highly reliable judges of pupils' writing. It is generally agreed that they are somewhat less confident and less reliable in judging pupils' speaking and listening. This is entirely understandable: speaking and listening are more ephemeral, and the criteria for making judgements about them are much less matters of common agreement. What would happen, then, if teachers took responsibility for making judgements about their pupils' reading, and made those judgements, not on the results of comprehension tests, but through observing reading processes and strategies in action? My guess is that at least initially, the reliability of their judgements would be lower than it is in making judgements about writing, but no lower than it is in making judgements for speaking and listening. The reason for this is related to the availability of the evidence upon which judgements are made. If teachers can see the texts with which the readers have been working, it will be easier to make judgements about the use of effective reading strategies. This small decrease in reliability, however, would be offset by a large increase in validity. If what we are seeking to capture is evidence about the generalisable strategies a reader uses, rather than their response to single texts, this is arguably what really matters in reading, and relates to those strategies and active approaches to text which readers need to take with them beyond school, and into adult life.

CHAPTER 6

Speaking and listening

In 1983, government funding was made available through the 'Lower Attaining Pupil Programme' (LAPP) for the establishment of an oracy project in Wiltshire. The project ran for seven years, joining up with the National Oracy Project when that began in 1987. At the time, there were very few markers that helped us to steer a course as we began to explore the possibilities for developing spoken language ability in the school years. Most research had taken place with pre-school children, and ideas about ability in oracy, especially in the secondary phase, were often limiting and superficial, based on predictions about what students **should** be achieving, rather than on any detailed studies into how they actually use the language. Assessment criteria, for example, that used in assessing students taking a City and Guilds 'Communication Skills' course, was often very crude and unrealistic:

Level 1 – To express and communicate feelings on a matter of personal concern.

Level 3 – To express and communicate convincingly feelings on matters of personal concern.

Level 5 – To express in some detail and communicate convincingly feelings and experience of personal and general concern.

Level 7 – To express feelings in detail and communicate sensitively the quality of experiences so that an effective and personal response is clearly evident.

'**Ability**' comes from the Latin word 'habilem' meaning 'having sufficient power...a capacity'. These definitions are useful when considering what 'ability' in the spoken language might mean. In this chapter I want to develop these interlocking notions of 'power over language' and 'the capacity' to use the language, because they seem to me to offer a perspective on the **development** of ability – as a capacity to be developed, extended, rather than as something fixed, something you are saddled with, unable to alter.

Light might be shed on what is known about ability in oracy by reviewing a little of the recent history of attitudes and thinking about the spoken language. Whilst thinking has undoubtedly moved on considerably, the establishment of a thorough working theory of spoken language development is still in its infancy. For example, only a few years ago, Janet Maybin was able to say:

> There is very little actually known, either about the structure, content and function of children's oral language, or about how it changes and develops over the school years. (Maybin 1991.)

> Level 9 – To express feelings and the quality of experiences evocatively and sensitively without confusion and with insight and self-awareness.

In this example, ability in oracy, or at least one aspect of it, is divided into a set of skills, increasing in difficulty, but detached from any consideration of **context.** Looking at this list of levels, one is forced to ask; 'what context?'; 'to whom?'; 'for what purposes?'. There may be, rarely, times when I can express my feelings 'evocatively and sensitively, without confusion and with insight and self-awareness', but I suspect that this is best left to the great poets! The point is that ability in the spoken language is **particularly** susceptible to fine tuned features of context – such as who's talking to whom, about what, where, and in what sort of power relationship.

More about this later. At this point, though, I want to sketch out some of the key shifts that have occurred in thinking about ability in oracy, recognising that, rather like layers of rock strata, recent additional insights can often lie thinly above deeper, more resistant notions.

1. Early Prescriptions

What little evidence there is of official attention to ability in the spoken language in the first part of this century reveals an emphasis on surface features, on the sounds of the language. The first time that the spoken language featured in an official report was in 1921. The Newbolt Report begins its section on oral language with this exhortation:

> Speech training must be undertaken at the outset. It is emphatically the business of the elementary school to teach all its pupils who either speak a definite dialect, or whose speech is disfigured by vulgarisms, to speak Standard English and to speak it clearly. (Board of Education 1921.)

The prevailing attitude at the time was to regard spoken language as a debased form of written language, and to measure speech by the standards one would expect of a piece of written text. This attitude was echoed twenty years later in the Norwood Report (1943): 'Habitual lip-laziness and disregard of final letters can be cured by a systematic campaign against them.'

2. Psycholinguistic Influences

The research of psychologists and linguists into early childhood development began to filter through to teachers in the late-1960s and early-1970s. A picture of the child as an active meaning maker and creative language user began to develop. However, one side effect of Chomsky's pioneering and influential work on language acquisition was the commonly held perception that the language system was pretty well complete by about the age of five.

3. Deficit Models

At about the same time, however, notions of 'verbal deficit' and 'language disadvantage' were becoming widely held. Many children were regarded as having 'little or no language' when they came to school, due to poor parenting, poverty, and other forms of social disadvantage. Schools and pre-school programmes such as 'Headstart' in the USA were expected to compensate by putting language in when it was missing.

4. Language Gaps

In recent years a different perspective has gradually gained ground, one which recognises **differences** in language use, not deficits. In part, this shift in attitude stems from the interest in children's spoken language that began when battery-operated tape recorders became more available and made field recordings of children's natural speech more accessible. Educationalists, as well as linguists, became interested in what children's talk revealed, and in the qualities of language that they showed themselves capable of producing. For example, Barnes, Britton and Rosen (1969) in *Language, the Learner and the School* offered a crucial insight. Many pupils in school, and in the secondary school in particular, found the language of education alienating, unfamiliar and unwelcoming, and retreated into inarticulacy, their language potential largely untapped, underused. As Rosen wrote (Barnes, Britton and Rosen (1969):

> Much of the language encountered in school looks at pupils across a chasm...Personal intellectual struggle is made irrelevant and the personal view never asked for. Language and experience are torn asunder. Worse still, many children find impersonal language mere noise. It is alien in its posture, conventions and strategies.

From the discourse analysts emerged a vivid picture of the 'situational constraints' of the classroom as far as genuine communication goes – a place where most of the spoken interaction is controlled by the teacher, and where 'communicative rights' are unequally distributed. The exciting revelations of the psycholinguists about the potential that children have for making meaning through talk was countered by the sociolinguists' findings that classrooms, and schools in general, were far from the best places for this to happen.

5. Official Sanctioning

Recent years have seen what is, on the surface at least, a dramatic turn around in the status of oracy in education. The Bullock Report *A Language for Life* (DES 1975) drew together many of the more recent insights that had begun to emerge from both sociolinguistics and the kinds of informed enquiry characterised by such groups as the London Association for the Teaching of English in the early 1970s. As a result, 'Language Across the Curriculum' became a 'movement' (and was also fiercely resisted and misunderstood in many schools). A decade after Bullock, the Kingman Committee of Enquiry (1988) recognised the value of classroom talk, and recommended that both the use, and the systematic study of spoken language should feature strongly in the curriculum.

The new National Curriculum took this view on board. From a position of relative neglect a decade or so ago, we are now in a situation where spoken language is equally weighted with reading and writing in National Curriculum English. Every primary school teacher, and every secondary English teacher, is in possession of a map of development (Attainment Target 1, and associated Statements of Attainment), and an equally extensive set of directions (Programmes of Study). They use these to ensure that the law is adhered to and that pupils should speak and listen through their compulsory schooling.

A more detailed look at developments in understanding of ability in the spoken language will help to illuminate some of the issues still surrounding the question of how best to define and promote ability in spoken English. In the early 1980s the Assessment of Performance Unit, for the purpose of national monitoring, created a taxonomy of speaking and listening, and used this to design assessment tasks. Significant features were on **purpose** and on **audience.** Their list of 'purposes' was as follows:

- Describing and explaining
- Informing/expounding
- Instructing/directing
- Reporting

- Narrating
- Arguing/persuading
- Discussing/collaborating
- Speculating/hypothesising. (APU 1982.)

Although they have been criticised for omitting the largely **interactive** nature of talk, establishing a model which over-emphasised the solo speaker or listener, there is no doubt that in generating a theory of oracy and a workable model of assessment, the APU increased our understanding about the **range** of ability that should be considered.

When the Cox Report (1989) first came out (Levels 1–5 only), its proposals for Attainment Target 1: Speaking and Listening drew on this **purposive** view of the spoken language. However, the requirement to place attainment in to a series of 'stepped' levels resulted in an over linear, and two dimensional view of the development of ability. For example, to attain:

Level 1 – Pupils should be able to speak freely, and listen, one-to-one to a peer group member.

Level 2 required: – In a range of activities (including problem solving), speak freely, and listen, to a small group of peers.

Level 4 – Speak freely and audibly to a class.

Level 5 – Speak freely and audibly to a larger audience of peers and adults.

Whilst offering an enlightened view of the **range** of purposes for talk, and the importance of **audience,** this early proposal from Cox fell into the trap of equating developing ability with speaking to increasingly larger and more unfamiliar audiences. By Level 5 the pupil was already required to speak to an audience larger than the size of a class. One wonders quite what Level 10 would have required! Fortunately, when the revised proposals were published, a more complex, subtle picture of development had emerged, which can be summarised as follows:

Development in Speaking and Listening is characterised by increasing:
- accuracy and precision
- ability to formulate complex instructions and questions
- ability to reformulate ideas
- ability to organise and sequence information
- ability to adjust language and delivery to suit audience and purpose
- ability to evaluate and reflect
- response to widening modes of address

– ability to collaborate

(Based on 'English From Ages 5-16, 1989)

The Cox Committee were open about the limitations of their model of oracy, recognising the absence of a well grounded theoretical base, and conscious that their proposals would need reviewing in the light of experience. In the Cox model, certain types of talking and listening are favoured above others – 'chairing' meetings rates higher than 'taking an active part in group discussions, showing sensitivity...' for example – and there is a strong argument that some of the oral abilities required to reach the higher levels favour pupils from certain backgrounds. Nevertheless, teachers do now have a useful set of grid references to help them chart a pupil's development over time, and across a range of different contexts.

Proposals for a revision of English from the National Curriculum Council (1993) put these recent gains into reverse, with the danger of precipitating a loss of the insights into pupils' spoken language and how it can be best promoted in schools. The proposals included the requirement that pupils 'should be taught to speak standard English', defined as 'the correct use of vocabulary and grammar'. The new proposals put greater emphasis as well on clarity and precision in speaking, and separate out 'listening' from 'communication'. The net result is a **reduced** view of ability in the spoken language, and a revival of some of the early prescriptions and deficit views.

There is a danger that the kinds of teacherly behaviour required to ensure that even young children are taught to speak Standard English will reinforce the alienating effect of some of school language, whilst having little or no positive effect on language use. It is significant that the reaction of both the teaching profession and also more widely – parents and industrialists, for example – was strongly opposed to these aspects of the proposals, and as a result some of the more damaging elements in the new proposals have been dropped – evidence surely of a growing consensus about the value of oracy.

So where are we now? I want to summarise what can confidently be asserted about ability in oracy that has either emerged gradually as part of the chequered history outlined earlier, or has been formulated more recently out of the endeavours of thousands of teachers in England and Wales who participated in the National Oracy Project (1987–1993).

1. Development in talk is primarily a case of extending the repertoire, becoming more versatile as a speaker and listener. A 'good' speaker and listener is flexible in his or her language use, able to adapt to the demands of different contexts. He or she is able to make informed choices over style, tone, and form of speech, according to an assessment of the **situation** (who am I talking to/with?); the **purpose** (what am I trying to achieve?); and the **topic** (what ideas am I trying to express?).

2. The development of this versatility can best happen in schools if pupils are encouraged to grapple with ideas and experiences through talk, and offered sympathetic, interested listeners. Two short examples will illustrate this point. In the first, Amy and Adam, both aged 5, have found a collection of shells in the sand tray, and are cleaning them at the sink. Their teacher joins in:

Teacher: Oh, look at the colours in this one! Doesn't that look better now it's clean? Look, you've got some shiny bits, and some dull bits. And what about this side? Look at these – do you know what shape that is?

Amy: Rainbowy.

Teacher: Hey, it does look like a rainbow, you're right.

Adam: When you go to Spain, don't go in the sea.

Teacher: Why?

Adam: Because they said on the telly that there's bad sea about in Spain.

Teacher: Is there? So you mustn't go in the sea?

Amy: We can go on the sand, Adam,...do you know, when I went in the sea on holiday it was all cold, so I ran out!

Teacher: Did you?

Adam: You can go in the pool.

The important thing to notice here is the role that the teacher adopts. Having initiated the discussion, presumably to prompt the children to explore the different shapes of the shells, she is prepared to act as a supportive conversational equal once Adam introduces the idea of the polluted sea. The result is that the children can take the conversational initiative and keep the talk flowing.

The second example, by way of comparison and contrast, took place in a Year 11 Environmental Studies class. The pupils had completed an assignment on one of a number of global environmental issues. They were then asked to prepare a short presentation on their issue, and to talk to a small group of other pupils who had each taken a different issue. Toby is introducing the topic of the 'Greenhouse Effect'. Here are two extracts, firstly from his opening (unscripted) talk, and then when he is being questioned by others in the group:

Toby: ...the impending Greenhouse Effect has only come to light recently, but the basic facts are: basically the earth has an atmosphere, which is a covering, like the glass of a greenhouse. It takes heat from the sun, comes in, hits the earth, then most of the heat is reflected back out into space, but the atmosphere traps a certain amount of the heat, keeping the temperature of the earth at a good temperature for all life to exist. But for 200 years or so since the industrial revolution, non-stop, countries around the world have been pumping out carbon dioxide, that's mainly from burning fossil fuels like coal and oil for power and in factories, and this excessive carbon dioxide is billowing up into the atmosphere and it's getting trapped there. Well the thing is, it traps more heat, so more heat is being trapped and less is getting out into space. So this causes the earth to warm up...
          (Section omitted)

Julie: So are pressure groups helping in this area?

Toby: Oh, very much, yeah. 'Cos it's fashionable to be green. Another gas which is affecting the atmosphere is CFCs – chloro-fluoro-carbons – which is a man-made gas, used in aerosols, hamburger cartons, fridges. It's a very small amount of this gas which is released, but the thing is, it's over two thousand times more potent than carbon dioxide, so it's affecting it so much. But now you get 'ozone-friendly' aerosols, where they've taken the CFCs out, they're trying to change hamburger cartons...

Toby is clearly a 'good' speaker, but this is not just a matter of innate language ability. The situation is working in his favour: he has a group of interested, knowledgeable listeners; he is talking on a topic in which he has a degree of expertise; the setting is informal; the task is clear to all; and once the initial presentation is over, interaction is encouraged. As a result, Toby is able to demonstrate, and in the process, continue to develop, his ability to explain, to sequence his ideas, to think on his feet, to respond to questions...

3. Whilst there is as yet no comprehensive, workable model of oracy and its assessment, any valid approach should include the following elements:

Meaning – the quality of thinking and feeling displayed:

- the ability to put language to use, across a range of functions
- the ability to create **joint** understanding
- the ability to listen and make sense of information

- the ability to formulate and reshape ideas and experience
- the ability to demonstrate knowledge and understanding through talk.

Development will involve more complex topics; greater objectivity of viewpoint and range of reference; use of own experience and ideas.

Interaction – how the pupil goes about talking and listening with others:

- the ability to work with others in different groupings
- the ability to be sensitive to the views and feelings of others
- the ability to take on a range of roles in a group.

Development will involve widening audiences and groupings, familiar and unfamiliar.

Language ('textual') features – what the pupil does with the language:

- the ability to make appropriate choices of vocabulary and syntax
- the ability to organise and structure information and ideas
- the ability to select stylistic features (figurative or rhetorical language, analogy, irony, humour, etc.)
- the ability to use the voice (intonation, pitch, pace, rhythm, volume, pauses, etc.)
- non-verbal features (gesture, facial expression).

Development will involve increasing control and choice over a widening range of features.

Awareness – what the pupil knows about spoken language:

- an awareness of one's own 'performance'
- an awareness of the 'ground rules' that operate in any given context
- an awareness of how others use language – how meanings are made, effects achieved
- an awareness of what constitutes 'appropriate' and 'inappropriate' spoken language.

Development will involve an increasing ability to self-monitor, to reflect and listen critically, and to use this reflection to improve 'performance'.

4. 'Good' talkers and listeners, then, will be reflective, self-aware language users. They will be able to stand back, with the help of their teachers, to consider their own use of language, to appraise and learn from it, and from the language of others, in ways that inform and influence future language use. Good assessment practice must therefore include a significant element of self-assessment and reflective discussion. This will, for example, involve pupils keeping 'talk diaries', using cassette tape recorders and video cameras, and discussing in advance of a task what **criteria** they should use to monitor and evaluate their own performance. Teachers will need to plan for this reflection, and model effective ways of talking about talk, responding to the pupils' comments in a positive way.

5. Effective teaching will be based on an understanding of the importance and influence of the context on spoken language. Teachers will need to plan for the conditions in which the 'peaks' of performance can occur. Supportive conditions include:

– a range of audiences
– responsive listeners
– talk being valued – especially the justification of opinions, the giving of explanations, the exploration of ideas, and the telling of stories
– supportive and, at times, challenging teacher roles, always as part of a collaborative relationship
– positive feedback to pupils
– carefully planned tasks which require a range of talk and create clear roles for pupils, including: expert; collaborator; interviewer; presenter; planner; arguer, etc.
– opportunities to reflect
– respect for language(s), including those for whom English is not the first language
– clearly defined, authentic purposes for talk
– pupils given responsibility for managing the talk
– topics for talk which draw on the pupils' own experience, and which encourage them to connect what they already know with new information and ideas.

6. Talk is often a window revealing other kinds of ability. It is often through talk that pupils reveal not just what they know or understand, but how they have organised information, how secure a grasp they have of it. Quite often, the very act of 'telling' others is a form of action on one's own understanding, helping to clarify, reject, sequence, and synthesise understanding. There are implications in this for teachers of all subjects.

Pupils can quite often say more than they might write; they might, through skilful questioning, reveal understanding or ability hitherto masked in their writing. The quality of a pupil's response to a poem, engagement in a science experiment, or appreciation of a skill in PE may often be more effectively communicated in spoken form. Teachers' assessments need to recognise this: what teachers in the Oracy Project came to call 'assessment **through** talk' to distinguish the purpose of the assessment from that of talk.

7. An education in oracy, planned to happen throughout the curriculum, will have a number of outcomes in mind:

- the capacity to use language, including standard English, flexibly to meet the demands of the workplace, future study, and the pupil's own needs and interests

- the capacity to continue to develop critical awareness of the ways others use spoken language to construct meaning and to influence others

- the capacity to use language creatively and imaginatively – to delight in language, and to value the artistic potential of the spoken word.

I began this chapter by reflecting on the meaning of the word 'ability', and have suggested that we need a more **expansive** version of the idea than is enshrined in the framework of current curriculum documents. There are many kinds of highly able spoken language users: those, for example, who can communicate their expertise clearly and helpfully; those who can listen and learn from what they hear; those who can talk others through crises, or lend a supportive ear; those who have no fear of asking difficult questions; storytellers and raconteurs; skilled group contributors; chairers of meetings; those who have learned how to stand up for their rights; deal with complaints; planners and presenters…the list is much longer than I have space for here. However, communicative rights are not equally distributed in our society – for reasons that are closely linked, for example, to class, gender, ethnicity, and educational opportunities. Certain kinds of speaking and listening are often regarded as having higher status than others; and some of those who possess many of the capacities listed above can still feel linguistically disadvantaged. Despite the advances that have been made in recent years, there is still an urgent need to offer all young people better **access** to **developed speaking and listening** in our schools. An effective education for the twenty-first century, with its need for flexible, adaptable, multiskilled, confident citizens, should be one which builds on the potential for language development that children bring with them into the classroom. If children's capacities as spoken language users are to be fully harnessed and developed, this will entail a radical shift in the patterns of communication which still persist in many classrooms.

Acknowledgement

To teachers and children at Bentley West School, Walsall, and Sheldon School, Wiltshire, for the two transcribed examples.

CHAPTER 7

Low-achievers in English

> Any examination in English embodies a view of language, however ill-defined, and conveys a view, however inarticulate, of how competence in language can be developed. Whether by inclusion, omission or emphasis these views point to ways of working in the classroom and to values and priorities.
> (LATE 1980.)

Definitions of what counts as ability and attainment are jointly construed, over time, by all members of a learning community. What it means to be literate depends on which literacies are valued; what it means to be a learner depends on the kinds of learning and learners valued. The GCSE gave English teachers more control over the creation of classroom learning communities, and as the definitions of what counts as ability and attainment in English were renegotiated in those classrooms, GCSE results improved (43.7% of candidates gained passes of C or above in 1988, 55% gained passes of C or above in 1992). Some children left the ranks of the low-achievers. Others remained, of course, because all examination systems exclude some people and define others as least successful. Yet many of those who remained in the ranks had their perceptions of what causes success and failure extended in ways that left them with more than low- and fixed-ability explanations for their relative low achievement.

'I'm not very good at English' as an hypothesis a child tests, or as a fact she accepts is, in effect, a triple whammy: it erodes self-worth; it undermines performance in many other curriculum areas and it jeopardises chances of success in the world that lies beyond school. What English teachers have discovered in recent years is that it is possible to create classroom learning communities – even within the constraints imposed by an examination system – where more children can safely test out hypotheses about their own abilities. It may be that if the National Curriculum Key Stage testing proposals had followed on from the CSE and GCE, the battles and campaigns would have been less vociferous – simply because there would have been less to defend.

Despite the gains, the GCSE, like its predecessors, has identified those who are excluded and those who are least successful. It may not be entirely helpful to think in terms of the 20% for whom the examination was not designed to cater when we are attempting to identify low-achievers and describe what is meant by low achievement in English. No arbitrary (or seemingly absolute) cut-off point – especially when it masks differences among pupils and schools – can serve the purpose. Nor would it be helpful to use the Warnock Report's identification of 20% of the school population with special educational needs (18% of whom are located in ordinary schools): it is true that all low-achievers have special, or unmet needs, but it is not true that all children with special educational needs are low-achievers in English.

The descriptions of GCSE candidates' attainments in English do, however, offer a partial picture of the characteristics of achievement at different levels and it may be that evidence of the achievements of the least successful allows us to make some inferences about the achievements of the excluded. The 1992 Examiners' Reports from NEAB, MEG and SEG identify weaker candidates who tend to:

● respond to texts by retelling stories, summarising plots, listing character traits and events;
● rely on anecdote, narrative and description;
● rehash material from given passages or from answers to questions already tackled;
● produce texts not governed by principles of organisation or cohesion;
● ignore or misinterpret instructions.

Examiners suggest that these candidates' achievements in coursework components of examinations can be restricted by:

● selection of inappropriate or inaccessible texts;
● too few opportunities for personal writing;
● the requirement to complete more pieces of coursework than the syllabus demands;
● the setting of imprecisely defined tasks, or tasks not carefully matched to abilities and aptitudes.

Knowing what some students do not do, or cannot do, as well as some other students should not lead us to make hasty conclusions about ability. An awareness of the characteristics of low achievement (however detailed or however described) is more valuable if informed by an awareness of the characteristics of low-achievers. The rationale for raising standards through the National Curriculum, its attendant assessment methodologies and reporting procedures, seems to be based on the erroneous view that a scarcity of rewards in a competitive climate will motivate children to try harder and thus achieve more. By mid-adolescence, most students have developed a less naïve view than this. Figure 1 is an attempt to describe the attainer's range of possible responses in a competitive climate where ability is narrowly defined and where rewards are scarce. We are indebted to Martin Covington (1992), whose work on motivational theory influenced our thinking about the characteristics of low-achievers.

Figure 1

Students should be able to:

Level 1: conclude from accumulated evidence that ability is low and will always be; expect failure in all situations and opt out entirely; find alternative sources of success and self-esteem.

Level 2: draw upon past experience to predict failure in all situations, and so avoid those situations where failure and its implications are to be demonstrated; conclude that it is dangerous to try because failure with effort proves low ability; adapt a defiant stance towards learning by discounting or undervaluing what is valued by those who succeed and those who confer success.

Level 3: anticipate failure in all new situations and be aware that nothing can be done to increase the likelihood of success; maximise teacher approval by adopting behaviours and attitudes that are valued; adapt a passive stance to learning, lower expectations and personal goals and be prepared to be controlled by others as a way of ensuring partial success.

Level 4: doubt own ability and approach tasks without the expectation of success; recognise that if success is achieved explanations other than high-ability ones will be available and that success is not a predictor of future success; appreciate that low effort explanations for failure are preferable to low ability ones, even if they are accompanied by teacher disapproval.

Level 5: acknowledge that ability may be either low or unchangeable, but possibly not both; doubt own ability and accept that it is sometimes unwise to try very hard because although it is not possible to avoid failure, it is possible to avoid the implications of failing despite having tried to succeed; recognise that success can be achieved though not necessarily repeated.

Level 6: acknowledge that ability may be neither low nor fixed; make considered decisions about preferred strategies on the basis that: (a) observable high effort followed by failure reduces teacher disapproval but confirms suspicions of low ability; (b) concealed high effort followed by success may give an impression of ability but it does not remove self-doubts; (c) low effort or apparent low effort masks the causes of failure; recognise that increased effort may be followed by success and that success may be a predictor of future success.

Level 7: have some confidence in own ability and approach tasks anticipating success; understand that learning strategies can affect outcomes and that new strategies can be acquired and developed; follow advice and instructions in an attempt to guarantee success and acknowledge that failure, if it occurs, is probably caused by factors other than low ability.

Level 8: conclude that ability is high and will remain so if coupled with effort; realise that experimentation, risk-taking and high expectations enhance learning; appreciate that effort followed by success leads to personal satisfaction and teacher approval.

Level 9: draw upon past experiences to anticipate success in all situations and approach new challenges with confidence; appreciate that failure is part of the learning process and that, properly interpreted, it can reveal ways of making further progress; be aware that lack of effort, like increased effort, can enhance beliefs of high ability.

Level 10: conclude from accumulated evidence that ability is high and will always be; expect success in all situations and plan for it; find additional kinds of success and sources of self-esteem.

The achievement dynamics for each child are, of course, unique and powerfully influenced by personal history. Yet schools and classrooms do shape the pattern of possible and permissible responses. The construct in Figure 1 – although it masks individual differences – offers a way of identifying the characteristics of low-achievers that may help to explain the characteristics of low achievement. Most low-achievers will be operating at Levels 1–4, where defences against past failures assure future failures. It is, coincidentally, hard to imagine how students possessing such characteristics could be expected to aspire beyond Level 4 on the National Curriculum attainment targets for English. The strategies they employ are qualitatively different from those available to other students.

The following snap-shot description illustrates how one student – who might be said to operate at Level 2 (Figure 1) – presents himself in English lessons.

Paul, a Year 8 student

The class had just finished reading Gene Kemp's novel *The Turbulent*

Term of Tyke Tyler. The students were offered a booklet of post-reading activities, designed to help them reflect upon the novel and make connections between the issues explored within it and their own experiences. In consultation with the teacher, the students were encouraged to select, from the range available, their activities for individual work. Paul, as ever, greeted the change of activity with enthusiasm (but his enthusiasm is invariably a short-lived celebration of escape from whatever went before). He made several false starts and numerous reselections before his teacher intervened in an attempt to guide his decision-making and encourage him to create a mental representation of a desired outcome towards which he could work. Paul finally agreed to work on a questionnaire about friendship, and the teacher agreed to act as scribe in order to remove (at least temporarily) the extraneous task demands.

She worked with him to create a structure for the questionnaire and, together, they began the process of brainstorming possible question types. The teacher's aim was to gradually release more and more responsibility for the work (and responsibility for the success of the outcome) to the student, but the student's aim was to refuse ownership. Initially he deferred to the teacher and welcomed her suggestions, but each time he was offered more responsibility for the work he deployed a new avoidance strategy – or a greater degree of commitment to an already-tried strategy. Perhaps aware of the teacher's determination to commit him to his assignment, and perhaps wishing to avoid her further attempts, Paul decided that he would finish the work on his own. The intervention ended. The student hastily completed the task, producing a piece of work with which neither he nor his teacher was satisfied.

Paul's next selected activity took him into a group where the contribution of each individual would influence the success of the shared outcome. He quickly alienated himself by refusing to co-operate and by making disparaging remarks about other members of the group. Again, he managed to avoid any sense of task ownership and sought, instead, refuge (and perhaps a vestige of success and a kind of approval?) in his oft-adopted role as class clown.

A week later, the class began reading *Gowie Corby Plays Chicken* and Paul informed everyone that Gowie marries Heather at the end. The teacher does not know if he intended to spoil his peers' enjoyment of the novel, or if he was displaying his knowledge for the approval of others – but she was relieved that he had not known how *The Turbulent Term of Tyke Tyler* would end.

As we all know, students' perceptions of themselves as learners are shaped and refined over time. By mid-adolescence most students have resolved any conflicts between how they see themselves as learners and how they believe they are seen by others: they are operating with their own informed personal theories of what counts as ability and attainment in different learning communities. Yet, as James Pye (1988) observed:

A teacher does not face individuals, but versions of individuals, versions tailored to suit the individual's particular needs, in a particular predicament of being in school. (Pye 1988, p.37.)

Rehearsed ways of presenting self, learned coping strategies and practised procedural displays reveal less about ability than about perceptions of ability. How teachers respond to 'versions of individuals' offers considerable scope for influencing personal theorizing and thus altering perceptions of ability and conceptions of what constitutes ability. Getting back to basics for students like Paul must mean altering such perceptions and conceptions.

Students' thinking about English

What follows is an account of a small-scale investigation into students' attitudes, interests and perceptions. In September 1993, 335 Year 8, 9 and 10 students from three comprehensive schools completed questionnaires which invited them to reflect upon their experiences of English up to that point. The first part of the questionnaire called for responses to twenty statements and pupils were offered a choice of five possible responses: Always, Usually, About Half the Time, Occasionally and Never. For reporting purposes these have been recorded in three categories: Always and Usually; About Half the Time; Occasionally and Never. The second part of the questionnaire gave students the opportunity to respond in writing. The prompt was: 'If a new pupil joined your class and asked **you** for advice about how to do well in **English,** what would you say? Please give as much advice as you can.' The questionnaires were administered by the students' usual English teachers during English lesson time. The students were told that they were being asked to take part in an investigation carried out by the writers, and that they were not expected to complete the questionnaire under test conditions, i.e. work in silence for a specified time. Students were not required to give names, but they were asked to indicate gender. Teachers were asked to identify low-achievers, using their own operational definitions rather than a given one. Approximately 26% of the students in each year group were identified as low-achievers.

The responses of identified low-achieving students and others were collated separately to allow comparisons of response across both ability and age ranges. (See Table 1.)

Table 1. *(The results are expressed as percentages.)*

	Always/Usually	About Half the Time	Occasionally/ Never	Always/Usually	About Half the Time	Occasionally/ Never	Always/Usually	About Half the Time	Occasionally/ Never
	YEAR 8			**YEAR 9**			**YEAR 10**		
1. I enjoy English									
Low-achievers	80	11	9	82	14	4	59	18	23
Others	85	9	6	77	18	5	68	25	7
2. I work hard in English									
Low-achievers	70	30	0	79	20	1	64	27	9
Others	83	13	4	89	6	5	87	12	1
3. My English teacher is pleased with my work									
Low-achievers	57	38	5	58	17	25	18	45	37
Others	78	16	6	71	18	11	57	31	12
4. I find the work in English easy									
Low-achievers	54	38	8	74	20	6	32	45	22
Others	82	9	9	72	21	7	42	43	15
5. I think I am good at English									
Low-achievers	49	40	11	54	29	17	36	27	36
Others	79	14	7	74	15	11	47	41	12

The pattern of responses to the first five questions indicates that low-achievers felt most positive about their experiences of English at the beginning of Year 9. Others felt most positive at the beginning of Year 8, but maintained generally more positive beliefs and attitudes than their low-achieving peers across the year groups. By the start of Year 10 a pattern emerges: identified low-achievers are considerably less positive than their counterparts in Years 8 and 9, and considerably less positive than other Year 10 pupils. Fewer enjoy English, fewer work hard, more are convinced that teachers are not pleased with their work and more have low opinions about their ability. There were no significant gender differences in the patterns of responses.

More low-achieving students – in all three years – enjoy independent work less than others do (and their enjoyment decreases over the years)

Table 2. *(The results are expressed as percentages.)*

	Always/Usually	About Half the Time	Occasionally/ Never	Always/Usually	About Half the Time	Occasionally/ Never	Always/Usually	About Half the Time	Occasionally/ Never
	YEAR 8			YEAR 9			YEAR 10		
6. I enjoy working on my own									
Low-achievers	57	11	32	37	10	53	32	31	36
Others	53	30	17	49	28	23	58	25	17
7. I enjoy working with a partner									
Low-achievers	75	19	6	93	6	1	86	9	4
Others	67	19	14	73	17	10	68	19	13
8. I enjoy working in small groups									
Low-achievers	76	13	11	66	24	10	67	22	10
Others	61	22	17	59	26	15	54	19	27
9. I enjoy talking in class discussion									
Low-achievers	49	16	34	58	20	22	68	18	14
Others	57	27	16	51	21	28	49	24	27
10. I enjoy listening in class discussion									
Low-achievers	67	16	17	65	14	11	63	23	14
Others	63	23	14	76	16	8	63	19	18

but they enjoy pair and small-group work more. (Table 2.) Their enjoyment of contributing to whole class discussions increases across the age groups, whilst the enjoyment of others decreases slightly. The majority of students, regardless of ability, continue to enjoy listening in class discussions. Collaborative work and opportunities for learning through talk are clearly valued by all pupils, but perhaps especially those who experience less success in other aspects of English work. One possible inference is that students identified as low-achievers – and many of the others who indicated that they never, or only occasionally, thought of themselves as good at English – draw evidence to suggest that English teachers are displeased with their work, not from collaborative activities but from the work they complete independently.

The low-achievers enjoy reading independently (like working alone in more general terms) less than others do, and the number of them finding it enjoyable decreases with age. (Table 3.) However, reading alone is generally regarded as more enjoyable than working alone for most pupils, regardless of ability. The implication here is that 'working on my own' is associated more with writing than with reading. Not surprisingly, low-

Table 3. *(The result are expressed as percentages.)*

	Always/Usually	About Half the Time	Occasionally/ Never	Always/Usually	About Half the Time	Occasionally/ Never	Always/Usually	About Half the Time	Occasionally/ Never
	YEAR 8			**YEAR 9**			**YEAR 10**		
11. I like reading quietly to myself									
Low-achievers	76	11	13	68	0	32	40	45	14
Others	79	9	12	71	13	16	73	10	17
12. I like reading to the rest of the class									
Low-achievers	22	16	62	34	17	49	9	23	68
Others	53	9	38	29	18	53	27	7	66
13. I like listening to the teacher read									
Low-achievers	65	16	19	72	10	18	27	37	36
Others	63	16	21	45	24	31	41	13	46
14. I like listening to other pupils read									
Low-achievers	49	29	22	63	27	10	37	41	22
Others	50	27	23	45	24	31	33	20	47
15. I understand what I read									
Low-achievers	81	16	3	73	10	17	78	18	4
Others	84	12	4	76	16	8	75	20	5

achievers, regardless of age (and many other students, especially at the beginning of Years 9 and 10) dislike reading aloud in classroom settings. The exposure this entails is, perhaps, threatening to many, but particularly threatening to those who are least confident and competent.

Enthusiasm for reading *per se* drops dramatically among low-achievers in Year 10, but for other students a growing negativity towards shared reading activities is counterbalanced by a continuing enjoyment of independent reading. Although all students retain a high level of confidence in their ability to understand what they read, it is unlikely that they all possess comprehension monitoring strategies of equal sophistication. The pattern of responses to this set of statements provides further evidence to suggest that low-achievers have their most positive perceptions and beliefs at the beginning of Year 9.

Yet by the beginning of Year 10 their perceptions and beliefs have altered: there is a sharp drop in the number of low-achievers who enjoy writing, like receiving assistance from English teachers and like giving assistance to their peers. (Table 4.) However, these students remain slight

Table 4. *(The result are expressed as percentages.)*

	Always/Usually	About Half the Time	Occasionally/Never	Always/Usually	About Half the Time	Occasionally/Never	Always/Usually	About Half the Time	Occasionally/Never
	YEAR 8			YEAR 9			YEAR 10		
16. I enjoy writing									
Low-achievers	59	24	22	62	10	28	41	41	18
Others	81	6	13	71	16	13	73	16	11
17. I like my teacher to help me with my writing									
Low-achievers	35	16	49	41	31	28	27	23	50
Others	26	16	58	34	14	52	37	16	47
18. I like other pupils to help me with my writing									
Low-achievers	11	24	65	27	5	68	24	22	54
Others	12	9	79	13	16	71	18	16	66
19. I like helping other pupils with their writing									
Low-achievers	22	11	67	49	10	41	18	32	49
Others	39	20	41	30	26	44	34	16	50
20. I like getting my work back when it has been marked by the teacher									
Low-achievers	78	10	12	73	6	21	73	0	27
Others	92	4	4	84	10	6	81	10	9

ly more positive than others do about receiving peer assistance. The perceived authority of the teacher as authentic audience and most constructive source of feedback is indicated by the responses given by all students to the final statement. The proportion of identified low-achievers who feel negative about this experience increases slightly over the years and is always higher than it is for other students. Nevertheless, the majority of students (irrespective of age or ability) remain positive about receiving teacher feedback – even though only 18% of the low-achievers and 57% of others in Year 10 believe that their English teacher is always or usually pleased with their work.

The general pattern of responses from all students shows that experiences of English in Year 9 were more critical for low-achieving students than for others: attitudes, perceptions and beliefs shaped during the year influenced their personal theorizing in negative ways. Some aspects of work in English seemed to be far more significant than others in shaping perceptions of low ability. Similar investigations in the future would, perhaps, reveal the extent to which these pupils' experiences of English at the end of Key Stage 3 were adversely affected by the fact that their teachers had less control than ever before over the creation of classroom learning communities, and over decisions about what counts as ability and attainment.

The second part of the questionnaire provided students with the opportunity to respond in writing to the prompt: *If a new pupil joined your class and asked* you *for advice about how to do well in* English, *what would you say? Please give as much advice as you can.* The vast majority of students, regardless of age or ability, gave advice relating to some or all of the following:

● listening to the teacher
● following instructions
● asking for assistance if it is required
● behaving well
● working hard
● completing work and handing it in on time
● paying attention to presentation, punctuation and spelling.

Students in Year 9 tended to proffer the same advice as younger students, but there was a greater emphasis on the importance of attitude and the avoidance of teacher disapproval. There was also more advice (especially from girls, regardless of ability or perceptions of ability) on how to achieve what teachers require. Students in Year 10 gave more varied advice and they tended to possess greater awareness of what doing well in English might mean.

The students described by their teachers as low-achievers did not offer advice distinctly different from the advice offered by other students: students' own perceptions of their abilities in English seemed far more significant. Although almost all of the students identified as low-achievers shared their teachers' perceptions of their ability, approximately 10% of others held low opinions of their own abilities in English. Students who held such perceptions tended to offer the least advice. Many of them, especially boys, but irrespective of age, wrote, not about the importance of behaving well, but about the importance of not behaving badly. One Year 9 boy wrote:

'You have to be quiet, do not swear, do not answer back, don't talk when the teacher is talking and keep yourself to yourself.'

Other students offered advice about behaviour, but it was rare for them to adopt (or echo?) such a tone of admonishment. This Year 9 boy's advice was more typical:

'Try as hard as you can and do things as good as you can. If anyone tries to distract you just ignore them. If anyone offers to you any help then just say no thank you. And try and do it yourself. Just try and get on the right side of the teacher. P.S. Behave.'

Almost all of the students identified as low-achievers (and approximately 80% of the others – a percentage that remained constant across the year groups) offered advice about writing. The advice offered by these two low-achieving Year 8 girls was repeated by many other students:

'To work your best and to make sure your spellings are correct.'

'In English you learn a lot example your handwriting spelling and also you must listen to the teacher.'

Their perceptions about how to do well in English may not be grossly inaccurate: it is what such students did not mention that reveals how inaccurate their perceptions may be. Most students acknowledged the importance of presentation and spelling, but the low-achieving students (particularly in Years 8 and 9) mentioned almost nothing else in relation to writing – apart from punctuation.

Advice offered by a more able Year 8 girl (who described herself as good at English in the first section of the questionnaire) reveals a more enabling set of perceptions. She wrote:

'...to think about what you write and to write it in detail, to imagine yourself being the person reading what you've written and write it in a style you enjoy. To be interested and enthusiastic in what you write.

To read with expression and characterisation. To take an interest in what other people think and say.

To be able to **spell quite** well.'

Interestingly, none of the students described by their teachers as low-achievers – and very few of the students who perceived themselves to be poor at English – offered advice that was subject-specific. It was only the more able student who wrote about how to do well in English as opposed to how to do well at school.

The sort of advice offered by these two Year 10 students, although different in significant ways, contains messages never found in the advice offered by low-achievers. Year 10 boy:

'Stick with your work. Don't lose concentration. When writing use as much emphasis and imagination as you can and have good relationships with everyone else in the lesson.'

Year 10 girl:

'...to do the work thoroughly and when you get it. When doing an essay first put down all of your ideas and do about two rough copies before putting in your final copy so that you can check all your spellings and make sure you've written about the right thing. Always ask your teacher questions when you need to and try and contribute in discussions in class. If you are nervous in reading aloud then do small parts and then increase.'

The messages are about confidence, valuing one's own ideas, the importance of strategies and participation. The students with poor perceptions of their abilities in English offered advice which revealed:

- limited and limiting ideas about how to do well in English;
- no awareness of how to make improvements in the aspects of English believed to be important;
- a lack of awareness about what distinguishes English from other subjects;
- no evidence to indicate awareness of how to take responsibility for learning, of how to plan, manage or evaluate what is done.

In fact, seven of these students responded to the request for advice with the words 'I don't know' and many others conveyed this message. These students are not operating as what Jerome Bruner calls members of 'the culture-creating community'; Bruner describes the learner's relationship to this community in the following way:

> If he fails to develop any sense of what I shall call reflective intervention in the knowledge he encounters, the young person will be operating continually from the outside in – knowledge will control and guide him. If he succeeds in developing such a sense, he will control and select knowledge as needed. If he develops a sense of self that is premised on his ability to penetrate knowledge for his own personal use, and if he can share and negotiate the result of his penetration, then he becomes a member of the culture-creating community. (Bruner 1986, p.132.)

The relative low-achievement of those who operate 'from the outside in' cannot be effectively addressed unless they are helped to develop more enabling perceptions, attitudes and beliefs. Past experiences cannot be changed, but the ways in which they are interpreted and allowed to influence future experiences can. Yet change cannot occur unless others allow it – and it cannot be sustained unless all members of the community possess broad conceptions of the kinds of learning and learner valued. If those who exist beyond, or on the fringes of, the culture creating community of the classroom are drawn in then the community itself is enriched.

English teachers involved with curriculum development projects of the late-1980s and early 1990s (most notably the National Writing Project, the National Oracy Project, the Technical and Vocational Education Initiative) made important discoveries about how the contexts for learning could be recast to the benefit of all students. Although such projects were distinct in important ways, they all had the following features in common:

- providing new purposes and new audiences that make linguistic and social demands on the communicative competences of learners;
- giving students greater access to the discourse communities that exist beyond the school, enabling them to experience the rhetorical demands and environmental realities of such communities;
- creating goal-directed, collaborative enterprises that require students to take more responsibility for their own learning, for devising and nego-tiating new learning styles and for planning, organising and evaluating what is achieved.

Such recasting resulted in more opportunities for students to wear the mantle of expert – often with recognition of and status being given to types of expertise formerly unacknowledged in classroom settings. It also led to more opportunities for students to act as participants, feeling the full, or only slightly tempered force of the consequences of their own actions. Thus, students were given new ways of appreciating the rele-vance of school learning and broader conceptions of the kinds of learning and learner valued both within their own recast communities and beyond. Typical projects – creating storybooks for younger audiences and produc-ing work experience logs and journals, for example – soon found popu-larity as GCSE coursework assignments. Many students who would have been defined as low-achievers by more narrow curriculum experiences gained enabling perceptions of what counts as ability and attainment. In many classrooms, the shift in goal orientation from performance in rela-tion to others, to success in relation to personal and shared aims, was accompanied by a redefinition of ability as a resource available to all, replenished by both individual and collective endeavours.

The belief that the needs of all individuals are best met through entitle-ment to a common curriculum is now widely held. It is a view expressed in the reports of Her Majesty's Inspectorate and in the National Curriculum Council's non-statutory guidance documents. An often-cited quotation appears in the Non-statutory Guidance for English:

> Participation in the National Curriculum by pupils with SEN is most likely to be achieved by encouraging good practice for all. Special educational needs are not just a reflection of pupils' inherent difficulties or disabilities; they are often related to factors within school which can prevent or exacerbate some problems. (C1.)

It is also a view shared by many of the educationists who have cam-paigned for a review of National Curriculum assessment arrangements.

The integration of students with special needs into mainstream schools, and the fuller integration of those members of the existing school community least well equipped to succeed in the school system, have led many English and Learning Support Departments to review their ways of working together. Success is no longer measured simply in terms of how effectively individual students are integrated into the ordinary life of the classroom, but also in terms of how effectively the curriculum, and its context, are adapted to make such integration possible.

In some schools English Departments have worked with Learning Support Departments to create learning-support bases. The Learning Support Base, with something to offer all students, is now a feature of such schools' provision and close liaison between the two departments ensures more flexible and responsive ways of working. The opportunity for withdrawal work with individuals and small groups remains, but with greater assurances that the support given relates closely to what is happening in the classroom and with less concern that the value of such support is counteracted by the stigma it traditionally attracts. In other schools, members of English Departments are developing their own shared expertise by working in learning support roles in one another's classrooms. The practice of English teachers team-teaching with colleagues from Learning Support Departments is a third model which is becoming increasingly common. What follows is a brief account of a course devised by one school as a way of formalising the links between these departments.

The Language Skills Course, Bemrose Community School, Derby

At the beginning of the 1993–94 academic year the number of English lessons for Years 7, 8 and 9 was increased from three to four fifty-minute periods each week. The additional timetable space was created to accommodate a course in language skills, jointly planned and team-taught by the English and Curriculum Support Departments. The departments felt that an emphasis on agreed and clearly defined skills work – as a separate but intrinsic element of English – would offer an opportunity for a rethink of both the focus and the methodology of skills teaching within the curriculum. In previous years the English Department had adopted an integrated approach to skills-based work, focusing on skills (though without an agreed definition) in response to the perceived needs of individuals and whole classes. Students with recognised special educational needs received additional support – both withdrawal and in-class – from the Curriculum Support staff.

The Language Skills Course adopted the tree as a logo. The skills it aims to develop are seen as part of a larger 'tree' of language, and the language tree is the metaphor students are offered as a way of thinking about language, and about their own developing competence as language users.

The course begins with an introductory phase designed to:

● clarify the nature and purpose of the course;
● introduce the five identified 'roots' of the language tree: spelling, punctuation, sentence-building, reading for meaning and word-power;
● describe the context for and contextualisation of skills work.

At the end of this phase students are invited to identify their own strengths and the areas of skills-based work they need to develop. Within each 'root' there are sub-divisions of activity and differing levels of complexity. For each area there is a range of worksheets and structured activities for students to choose from. The selection is made on the basis of identified need. The two teachers collaborate to create resources matched to the needs of each student and share responsibility for ensuring that students' goal-setting is realistic – that their goals are meaningful, time-bound, specific and attainable. Students are given control over the pace and direction of learning: they negotiate and plan their own individual journeys along the roots and record their progress by shading in areas on root maps. Progress is not bound up with ability – two students might develop or refine a skill but at different levels of sophistication. The students establish their own targets (or mastery goals) and performance is evaluated in terms of how successfully these are met.

The course team recognises the importance of embedding skills-work in appropriate texts and contexts: texts from different curriculum areas can be brought into the course; the opportunities for students to transfer their newly-acquired skills (or abilities to work to higher levels of competence) across contexts are assured by the English Department working closely with the Curriculum Support Department, which, in turn, works closely with other Departments.

As English and Learning Support Departments renegotiate ways of working together and evolve different modes of collaboration the scope for developing new forms of shared expertise increases, so too does the scope for finding new answers to old questions.

The process of recasting the context for learning – like the process of redefining the curriculum – creates new ways of defining what counts as success and new ways of shaping perceptions of ability. The greater the number of students who benefit, the more confident we should be about the value of what has been created. When deciding where to go next we should look to those who have gained least, for it is from them that we can learn most.

References

Adams, A. and Pearce, A. (1974) *Every English Teacher*. Oxford: Oxford University Press.

Adelman, C. (1976) 'Mixed Ability Classes – some typical problems', *Cambridge Journal of Education*, 6.

Ainscow, M. and Tweddle D.A. (1988) *Encouraging Classroom Success*. London: David Fulton Ltd.

Andrews, R. (1989) *Narrative and Argument*. Milton Keynes: Open University Press.

Andrews, R. (1991) *The Problem with Poetry*. Milton Keynes: Open University Press.

Andrews, R. et al (1993) *Improving the Quality of Argument, 5-16*, Final Report, University of Hull.

Appleyard, J.A. (1990) *Becoming a Reader*. Cambridge: Cambridge University Press.

APU (1981) *Language Performance in Schools*, Primary Report No. 1. London: HMSO.

APU (1982) *Language Performance in Schools*, Secondary Survey Report No. 1. London: HMSO.

APU (1983) *How Well can 15-year-olds Write?* DES.

Bailey, C. and Bridges, D. (1983) *Mixed Ability Grouping – A Philosophical Perspective*. London: George Allen and Unwin.

Bailey, M. (1993) 'Children's Response to Fiction', M.Ed. dissertation, Nottingham University.

Barnes, D. (1976) *From Communication to Curriculum*. London: Penguin.

Barnes, D., Britton, J. and Rosen, H. (1969) *Language, the Learner, and the School*. London: Penguin.

Barrs, M. (1990) *Words Not Numbers: Assessment In English*. Exeter: Short Run Press, National Association of Advisers in English and The National Association for the Teaching of English.

Becher, A. (1987) 'Disciplinary discourse', *Studies in Higher Education*, **12**(3).

Becher, A. (1989) *Academic Tribes and Territories*. Milton Keynes: Open University Press.

Benton, M. (1988) *Young Readers Responding to Poems*. London: Routledge.

Bereiter, C. (1980) 'Development in Writing', in L.W. Gregg and E.R. Steinberg (Eds) *Cognitive Processes in Writing*. Hillsdale, New Jersey: Erlbaum.

Beveridge, S. (1993) *Special Educational Needs in Schools*. London: Routledge.

Board of Education (1921) *The Teaching of English in England* (The Newbolt Report). London: HMSO.

Boomer, G. (1985) *Fair Dinkum Teaching and Learning, Reflections on Literacy and Power*. New Jersey: Boynton/Cook.

Boyd, W. (1924) *Measuring Devices in Composition, Spelling and Arithmetic*. London: Harrap.

Briggs, D. (1980) 'A study of the influence of handwriting upon grades using examination scripts', *Educational Review*, **32**(2), pp.185–93.

Britton, J. et al (1966) *Multiple Marking of English Compositions*. London: HMSO.

Britton, J. et al (1975) *The Development of Writing Abilities (11–18)*. Basingstoke: Macmillan.

Bruner, J. (1986) *Actual Worlds, Possible Minds*. Cambridge, MA: Harvard University Press.

Bullock, A. (1975) *A Language for Life*. London: HMSO.

Chater, P. (1984) *Marking and Assessment in English*. London: Methuen.

Christie, F. (1987) 'Genres as choice', in Ian Reid *The Place of Genre in Learning: Current Debates*. Victoria, Australia: Deakin University.

Cooper, C.R. and Odell, L. (1977) *Evaluating Writing: Describing, Measuring, Judging*. Urbana, Illinois: NCTE.

Covington, M.V. (1992) *Making the Grade. A self-worth Perspective on Motivation and School Reform*. Cambridge: Cambridge University Press.

Czerniewska, P. (1992) *Learning about Writing*. Oxford: Blackwell.

Dearing, R. (1993) *The National Curriculum and its Assessment*. London: School Curriculum and Assessment Authority.

Dearing, R. (1993) *The National Curriculum and its Assessment: an interim report*. London: NCC and SEAC.

Department for Education (1993) *English for Ages 5–16* London: HMSO.

Department for Education (1993) *English for Ages 5–16* – Proposals of the Secretary of State for Education and the Secretary of State for Wales. London: HMSO.

Department of Education and Science (1975) *A Language for Life* (The Bullock Report). London: HMSO.

Department of Education and Science (1987) *Teaching Poetry in the Secondary School: an HMI view*. London: HMSO.

Department of Education and Science (1989) *English for ages 5–16* (The Cox Report). London: HMSO.

Diederich, P.B. (1966) 'How to measure growth in writing ability', *English Journal*, **55**, pp.435–449.

Dixon, J. and Stratta, L. (1982) *Teaching and assessing argument*. Birmingham: Birmingham University.

Dixon, J. and Stratta, L. (1986) *Writing Narrative – and Beyond*. Ottawa:

Canadian Council of Teachers of English.

Dockrill, J. and McShane J., (1993) *Children's Learning Difficulties. A Cognitive Approach*. Oxford: Blackwell.

Dole, J.A., Duffy, G.G., Roehler, L.R. and Pearson, P.D. 'Moving from the old to the new: Research on reading comprehension instruction', *Review of Educational Research*, **61**(3), p.239–264.

Eagleton, T. (1983) *Literary Theory: an introduction*. Oxford: Blackwell.

Fish, S. (1980) *Is there a Text in this Class?* Cambridge, MA: Harvard University Press.

Freedman, A. and Pringle, I. (1984) 'Why students can't write arguments', *English in Education*, **18**(2), pp.73–84.

Gilbert, P. (1992) 'Voice/text/pedagogy: re-reading the writing classroom', in Andrews R., *Rebirth of Rhetoric*. London: Routledge.

Goodwyn, A. (1992) 'Theoretical Models of English Teaching', *English in Education*, **26**(3).

Goodwyn, A. (1993) '*The Reading History of English Teachers*', unpublished paper given at the NCTE, Assembly on Research Conference, Chicago.

Graves, D. and Sunstein, B. (1992) *Portfolio Portraits*. Portsmouth, NH: Heinemann.

Gregory, R.P. (1986) 'Mixed Ability Teaching – A Rod for the Teacher's Back?' *Journal of Applied Educational Studies*, **15**(2), Winter, pp. 56-62.

Harpin, W.S. (1976) *The Second 'R': Writing development in the Junior School*. London: Allen and Unwin.

Harrison, B.T. (1986) *Sarah's Letters: A Case of Shyness*. London: Institute of Education, London University.

Heath, S.B. (1983) *Ways with Words*. Cambridge: Cambridge University Press.

HMI (1978) *Mixed Ability Work in Comprehensive Schools*. London: HMSO.

Hunt, K.W. (1970) *Syntactic Maturity in School Children and Adults*. Chicago: Chicago University Press.

ILEA (1976) *Mixed Ability Grouping*. Report of an ILEA Inspectorate survey. London: ILEA.

Johnston, B. (1987, Rvsd Edn.) *Assessing English: helping students to reflect on their work*. Milton Keynes: Open University Press.

Johnston, P. 'Assessment as social practice. National Reading Conference annual review of research' in D.J. Leu and C.K. Kinzer (Eds) (1993) *Examining Central Issues in Literacy Research, Theory and Practice*. Forty-second Yearbook of the National Reading Conference. Chicago: National Reading Conference.

Kelly, A.V. (1974) *Teaching Mixed Ability Classes*. London: Harper and Row.

Kelly, A.V. (1978) *Mixed Ability Grouping*. London: Harper and Row.

Kinneavy, J. (1971) *A Theory of Discourse*. Englewood Cliffs, New Jersey: Prentice Hall.

LATE (1965) *Assessing Compositions*. Glasgow: Blackie.

Levine, K. (1986) *The Social Context of Literacy*. London: Routledge and Kegan Paul.

Loban, W. (1963) *The Language of Elementary School Children*. Urbana, Illinois: NCTE.

Loban, W. (1976) *Language Development: Kindergarten through grade 12*. Urbana, Illinois: NCTE.

London Association for the Teaching of English (1980) *English Exams at 16+*. London: LATE.

Lunzer, E. and Gardner, K. (Eds) (1979) *The Effective Use of Reading*. London: Heinemann.

Lunzer, E., Gardner, K., Davies, F. and Greene, T. (1984) *Learning From the Written Word*. Edinburgh: Oliver and Boyd.

Maimon, E.P. (1983) 'Maps and genres', in Horner, W.B. (Ed) *Composition and Literature, Bridging the Gap*. Chicago: Chicago University Press.

Mais, S.P.B. (1914) *Journal of English Studies*, **2**(3).

Marenbon, J. (1987) *English, our English*. London: Centre for Policy Studies.

Marshall, H.H. (Ed) (1990) *Redefining Student Learning. Roots of Educational Change*. New Jersey: Ablex.

Maybin, J. (1991) 'Children's Informal Talk and the Construction of Meaning', in *English in Education* 25 (NATE). The National Oracy Project – for a thorough account of the kinds of thinking and development, see Norman, K. (Ed) (1992) Thinking Voices. London: Hodder and Stoughton.

MEG (1992) Report on the Examination in English, Syllabus Code 1500, 1501, 1505, 1506. Summer.

Miller, J.H. (1983) 'Composition and Decomposition', in Winifred Bryan Horner (Ed) *Composition and Literature, Bridging the Gap*. Chicago: Chicago University Press.

Mills, R. (1977, 1987, Rvsd Edn) *Teaching English to all*. London: Robert Royce.

Ministry of Education (1963) *Half our Future* (The Newsom Report). London: HMSO.

Moffett, J. (1968) *Teaching the Universe of Discourse*. Mifflin Co, Boston: Houghton.

Moriarty, H. (1987) 'Screaming for Streaming', *Times Educational Supplement*, March, p.27.

National Curriculum Council (1989) *A Curriculum for All*. York: NCC.

National Curriculum Council (1990) *Non-statutory Guidance, English*. York: NCC.

National Curriculum Council (1991) *National Oracy Project, Teaching Talking and Learning in Key Stage Three*. York: NCC.

National Curriculum Council (1992), *National Curriculum English: The case for revising the order*. York: NCC.

National Curriculum Council (1993) *English for Ages 5 to 16 (1993)*. York: NCC.

NEAB (1992) Report on the CGSE Examination. English Syllabus A, B, C English Literature syllabuses A and B, English and English Literature (Dual Certificate). NEAB.

Neville, M. (1988) *Assessing and Teaching Language*. Basingstoke: Macmillan Education.

Newbold, D. (1977) *Ability Grouping – The Banbury Inquiry*. Windsor: NFER.

NFER (1981) *Mixed Ability Teaching*. Windsor: NFER-Nelson.

Peers, E.A. (1914) *Journal of English Studies*, **3**(1).

Peters, M. (1985) *Spelling: Caught or Taught? A New Look*. London: Routledge.

Protherough, R. (1978) 'When in doubt, write a poem', *English in Education*, **12**(1), pp.9–21.

Protherough, R. (1983) *Developing Response to Fiction*. Milton Keynes: Open University Press.

Protherough, R. (1983) *Encouraging Writing*. London: Methuen.

Protherough, R. (1986) *Teaching Literature for Examinations*. Milton Keynes: Open University Press.

Protherough, R. (1989) *Students of English*. London: Routledge.

Pumfrey, P.D. and Elliot, C.D. (1990) *Children's Difficulties in Reading, Spelling and Writing. Challenges and Responses*. Basingstoke: The Falmer Press.

Purves, A.C. (1992) *The IEA Study of Written Composition II: Education and Performance in Fourteen Countries*. Oxford: Pergamon Press.

Pye, J. (1989) *Invisible Children. Who are the real losers at school?* Oxford: Oxford University Press.

Reid, I. (1987) *The Place of Genre in Learning*. Victoria, Australia: Deakin University.

School Curriculum and Assessment Authority (1994) *English in the National Curriculum, Draft Proposals*. London: HMSO.

SEG. Chief Examiners' Reports, English and English Literature, Summer, 1992.

Stedman, L.C. and Kaestle, C.F. 'Literacy and reading performance in the United States, from 1880 to the present', *Reading Research Quarterly*, **22**(1), p.8–46.

The *Norwood Report* (1943). London: HMSO.

The Wiltshire Oracy Project – see Howe, A. (1992) *Making Talk Work*. London: Hodder and Stoughton.

Thomson, J. *Understanding Teenagers' Reading*. Norwood: Australian Association for the Teaching of English.

Thornton, G. (1986) *APU Language Testing 1979–1983*. DES.

Tierney, R., Carter, M. and Desai, L. (1991) *Portfolio Assessment in the Reading-writing Classroom*. Norwood, MA: Christopher Gordon.

Wade, B. and Moore, M. (1993) *Experiencing Special Education. What Young People with Special Educational Needs Can Tell Us*. Milton Keynes: Open University Press.

Walsh, B. (1989) *My Language, Our Language: Meeting Special Needs in English 11–16*. London: Routledge.

Wesdorp, H. et al (1982) 'Towards a conceptualisation of the scoring of written composition', *Evaluation in Education*, **5**.

White, E.M. (1985) *Teaching and Assessing Writing*. San Francisco: Jossey-Bass.

White, J. (1986) *The Assessment of Writing: Pupils aged 11 and 15*. Windsor: NFER-Nelson.

Widlake, P. (1983) *How to Reach the Hard to Teach*. Milton Keynes: Open University Press.

Wilkinson, A. (1986) *The Quality of Writing*. Milton Keynes: Open University Press.

Williams, J. (1979) 'Defining Complexity', *College English*, **40**(6), pp.595–609.

Wood, R. and Napthali, W.A. (1975) 'Assessment in the classroom: what do teachers look for?', *Educational Studies*, **1**(3), pp.151 ff.

Yorke, M. (1974) *English in Education,* **8**(2).

Yorke, M. (1979) *Use of English,* **29**(3).

Young, P. and Tyre, C. (1992) *Gifted or Able*. Milton Keynes: Open University Press.

Zelan, K. (1991) *The Risks of Knowing. Developmental Impediments to School Learning.* New York: Plenum Press.

Index

128

Peters, 9
poetry, 2, 3
Pringle, 55
Protherough, 1-5, 7, 15, 49-51, 56, 58, 74-75, 79-80
Purves, 50, 65
Pye, 107

reader response, 4, 53
reading, 12, 17-20, 51-53, 68-89
Reid, 55
Roehler, 83-86
Romantic Movement, the 5
Rosen, 92

Shakespeare, 6, 7
Southern Examination Group, 103
Speaking and Listening, 1, 6, 12, 17-18, 22-23, 26, 38, 68, 90-101
spelling, 9, 10, 17, 20, 22, 26, 61, 113
Standard English, 6, 8, 53, 61, 95
Stedman, 83
Stratta, 59
Sunstein, 67

Technical Vocational Education Initiative, 115
Thomson, 4
Thornton, 52
Tierney, 67
Tyre, 14

Warnock Report, The 103
Wesdorp, 54
White, 50, 51, 52
Wilkinson, 60
Williams, 59
Wood, 56
writing, 1, 2, 12, 17, 20, 47-65

Yorke, 7
Young, 14